MARRIAGE (SAME SEX COUPLES) ACT 2013 (UK)

Updated as of March 26, 2018

THE LAW LIBRARY

TABLE OF CONTENTS

Introductory Text

Marriage (Same Sex Couples) Act 2013

2013 CHAPTER 30

An Act to make provision for the marriage of same sex couples in England and Wales, about gender change by married persons and civil partners, about consular functions in relation to marriage, for the marriage of armed forces personnel overseas, for permitting marriages according to the usages of belief organisations to be solemnized on the authority of certificates of a superintendent registrar, for the review of civil partnership, for the review of survivor benefits under occupational pension schemes, and for connected purposes.

[17th July 2013]

Be it enacted by the Queen's most Excellent Majesty, by and with the advice and consent of the Lords Spiritual and Temporal, and Commons, in this present Parliament assembled, and by the authority of the same, as follows:—

Modifications etc. (not altering text)

C1. Act modified by SI 1995/866, reg. 2. B(4) (as inserted (E.W.S.) (13.3.2014) by The National Health Service Pension Scheme, Additional Voluntary Contributions, Compensation for Premature Retirement and Injury Benefits (Amendment) Regulations 2014 (S.I. 2014/78), regs. 1. (2), 26)

C2. Act modified by SI 2002/1311, reg. 2. A(4) (as inserted (E.W.S.) (13.3.2014) by The National Health Service Pension Scheme, Additional Voluntary Contributions, Compensation for Premature Retirement and Injury Benefits (Amendment) Regulations 2014 (S.I. 2014/78), regs. 1. (2), 23)

C3. Act modified by SI 2008/653, reg. 2.A.1. A(4) (as inserted (E.W.S.) (13.3.2014) by The National Health Service Pension Scheme, Additional Voluntary Contributions, Compensation for Premature Retirement and Injury Benefits (Amendment) Regulations 2014 (S.I. 2014/78), regs. 1. (2), 12)

C4. Act modified by SI 2000/619, reg. 2. A(4) (as inserted (E.W.S.) (13.3.2014) by The National Health Service Pension Scheme, Additional Voluntary Contributions, Compensation for Premature Retirement and Injury Benefits (Amendment) Regulations 2014 (S.I. 2014/78), regs. 1. (2), 19)

C5. Act modified by SI 2008/653, reg. 3. A.1. A(4) (as inserted (E.W.S.) (13.3.2014) by The National Health Service Pension Scheme, Additional Voluntary Contributions, Compensation for Premature Retirement and Injury Benefits (Amendment) Regulations 2014 (S.I. 2014/78), regs. 1. (2), 15)

C6. Act modified by SI 1995/300, reg. A4. (4) (as inserted (E.W.S.) (13.3.2014) by The National Health Service Pension Scheme, Additional Voluntary Contributions, Compensation for Premature Retirement and Injury Benefits (Amendment) Regulations 2014 (S.I. 2014/78), regs. 1. (2), 4)

Spread sheet - Statistics

Collection Ordered   Pick-up
_____   _____
                      No.   No
                      Boxes   Folders
                      _____   _____

Recorded   Recorded
ARC Numbers   ARC Numbers
on Boxes   or Folders
_____   _____
                                        Collection   Collection
                                        Names   Started
                                        in ROW   _____
                                        _____

Collection   Collection **
Processed   Completed
_____   _____
                                        Collection
                                        Working on
                                        _____

PART 1. Marriage of same sex couples in England and Wales

PART 1 Marriage of same sex couples in England and Wales

1. Extension of marriage to same sex couples

(1) Marriage of same sex couples is lawful.

(2) The marriage of a same sex couple may only be solemnized in accordance with—

    (a) Part 3 of the Marriage Act 1949,

    (b) Part 5 of the Marriage Act 1949,

    (c) the Marriage (Registrar General's Licence) Act 1970, or

    (d) an Order in Council made under Part 1 or 3 of Schedule 6.

(3) No Canon of the Church of England is contrary to section 3 of the Submission of the Clergy Act 1533 (which provides that no Canons shall be contrary to the Royal Prerogative or the customs, laws or statutes of this realm) by virtue of its making provision about marriage being the union of one man with one woman.

(4) Any duty of a member of the clergy to solemnize marriages (and any corresponding right of persons to have their marriages solemnized by members of the clergy) is not extended by this Act to marriages of same sex couples.

(5) A "member of the clergy" is—

    (a) a clerk in Holy Orders of the Church of England, or

    (b) a clerk in Holy Orders of the Church in Wales.

Commencement Information

I1. S. 1 in force at 13.3.2014 by S.I. 2014/93, art. 3. (a)

Religious protection

2. Marriage according to religious rites: no compulsion to solemnize etc

(1) A person may not be compelled by any means (including by the enforcement of a contract or a statutory or other legal requirement) to—

    (a) undertake an opt-in activity, or

    (b) refrain from undertaking an opt-out activity.

(2) A person may not be compelled by any means (including by the enforcement of a contract or a statutory or other legal requirement)—

    (a) to conduct a relevant marriage,

    (b) to be present at, carry out, or otherwise participate in, a relevant marriage, or

    (c) to consent to a relevant marriage being conducted,

where the reason for the person not doing that thing is that the relevant marriage concerns a same sex couple.

(3) In this section—

"opt-in activity" means an activity of the kind specified in an entry in the first column of the following table which falls to be undertaken for the purposes of any enactment specified in the corresponding entry in the second column;

"opt-out activity" means an activity which reverses, or otherwise modifies, the effect of an opt-in activity.

Activity | Enactment |

— Any of these provisions of the 1949 Act:
  - section 26. A(3);
  - section 26. B(2), (4) or (6);
  - section 44. A(6);
  - section 46. (1. C)

— Regulations under section 70. A(5) of the 1949 Act (as mentioned in section 70. A(6)(c) of that Act) relating to an application for registration

— Section 1. (3) of the Marriage (Registrar General's Licence) Act 1970

— An armed forces overseas marriage Order in its application to marriages of same sex couples (as mentioned in paragraph 9. (5) of Schedule 6)

Applying for the registration of a building | Section 43A of the 1949 Act |

Authorising a person to be present at the solemnization of marriages of same sex couples in a building registered under section 43A of the 1949 Act | Section 43B of the 1949 Act |

Being authorised to be present at the solemnization of marriages of same sex couples in a building registered under section 43A of the 1949 Act | Section 43B of the 1949 Act |

Any of these provisions of the 1949 Act:
  - section 43. A(3);
  - section 43. B(2);
  - section 44. A(7)

(4) In this section—

"1949 Act" means the Marriage Act 1949;

"armed forces overseas marriage Order" means an Order in Council under Part 3 of Schedule 6;

"person"—
  - includes a religious organisation;
  - does not include a registrar, a superintendent registrar or the Registrar General;

"relevant marriage" means—
  - a marriage of a same sex couple solemnized in accordance with—

section 26. A or 26. B of the 1949 Act (marriage in a place of worship or in another place according to religious rites or usages),

Part 5 of the 1949 Act (marriage in a naval, military or air force chapel),

section 1 of the Marriage (Registrar General's Licence) Act 1970 (deathbed marriage), where the marriage is according to religious rites or usages, or

an armed forces overseas marriage Order, where the marriage is according to religious rites or usages,
  - including any ceremony forming part of, or connected with, the solemnization of such a marriage; and
  - a marriage ceremony read or celebrated in accordance with section 46 of the 1949 Act in respect of a same sex couple (religious ceremony after registrar's marriage of same sex couple); and a reference to conducting a relevant marriage is to be read accordingly.

(5) In section 110 of the Equality Act 2010 (liability of employees and agents), after subsection (5) insert—

"(5. A)A does not contravene this section if A—
  (a) does not conduct a relevant marriage,
  (b) is not present at, does not carry out, or does not otherwise participate in, a relevant marriage, or
  (c) does not consent to a relevant marriage being conducted,
for the reason that the marriage is the marriage of a same sex couple.

(5. B)Subsection (5. A) applies to A only if A is within the meaning of "person" for the purposes of section 2 of the Marriage (Same Sex Couples) Act 2013; and other expressions used in subsection (5. A) and section 2 of that Act have the same meanings in that subsection as in that

section.".

(6) In Schedule 3 to the Equality Act 2010 (services and public functions: exceptions), after Part 6 insert—

"PART 6. A Marriage of same sex couples in England and Wales

25. A(1)A person does not contravene section 29 only because the person—

(a) does not conduct a relevant marriage,

(b) is not present at, does not carry out, or does not otherwise participate in, a relevant marriage, or

(c) does not consent to a relevant marriage being conducted,

for the reason that the marriage is the marriage of a same sex couple.

(2) Expressions used in this paragraph and in section 2 of the Marriage (Same Sex Couples) Act 2013 have the same meanings in this paragraph as in that section.".

Commencement Information

I2. S. 2 in force at 13.3.2014 by S.I. 2014/93, art. 3. (a)

Part 3 of the Marriage Act 1949.

3. Marriage for which no opt-in necessary

In Part 3 of the Marriage Act 1949, for section 26 substitute—

"26. Marriage of a man and a woman; marriage of same sex couples for which no opt-in necessary

(1) The following marriages may be solemnized on the authority of two certificates of a superintendent registrar—

"(a)a marriage of a man and a woman, in a building registered under section 41, according to such form and ceremony as the persons to be married see fit to adopt;

(b) a marriage of any couple in the office of a superintendent registrar;

(bb) a marriage of any couple on approved premises;

(c) a marriage of a man and a woman according to the usages of the Society of Friends (commonly called Quakers);

(d) a marriage between a man and a woman professing the Jewish religion according to the usages of the Jews;

(dd) a qualifying residential marriage;

(e) a marriage of a man and a woman according to the rites of the Church of England in any church or chapel in which banns of matrimony may be published."

(2) In this section "qualifying residential marriage" means—

(a) the marriage of a man and a woman (other than a marriage in pursuance of subsection (1)(c) or (d) above), one or each of whom is house-bound or a detained person, at the usual place of residence of the house-bound or detained person or persons, or

(b) the marriage of a same sex couple (other than a marriage according to the rites of the Church of England or other religious rites or usages), one or each of whom is house-bound or a detained person, at the usual place of residence of the house-bound or detained person or persons.".

Commencement Information

I3. S. 3 in force at 13.3.2014 by S.I. 2014/93, art. 3. (a)

4. Opt-in: marriage in places of worship

(1) After section 26 of the Marriage Act 1949 insert—

"26. AOpt-in to marriage of same sex couples: places of worship

(1) A marriage of a same sex couple in an appropriately registered building according to such form and ceremony as the persons to be married see fit to adopt may be solemnized on the authority of two certificates of a superintendent registrar.

(2) For the purposes of this section "appropriately registered building" means a building which has been registered under section 43. A.

(3) An application for registration of a building under section 43. A may not be made unless the relevant governing authority has given written consent to marriages of same sex couples.

(4) For that purpose, in relation to a building—

"relevant governing authority" means the person or persons recognised by the members of the relevant religious organisation as competent for the purpose of giving consent for the purposes of this section;

"relevant religious organisation" means the religious organisation for whose religious purposes the building is used.

(5) Nothing in this section is to be taken to relate or have any reference to marriages solemnized according to the rites of the Church of England.

(6) This section is subject (in particular) to sections 44. A to 44. C (registration of shared buildings for marriage of same sex couples) and regulations made under any of those sections.".

(2) Schedule 1 (registration of buildings etc) has effect.

Commencement Information

I4. S. 4 in force at 31.10.2013 for specified purposes by S.I. 2013/2789, art. 2. (a)

I5. S. 4 in force at 13.3.2014 in so far as not already in force by S.I. 2014/93, art. 3. (b)

5. Opt-in: other religious ceremonies

After section 26. A of the Marriage Act 1949 insert—

"26. BOpt-in to marriage of same sex couples: other religious ceremonies

(1) A marriage may, in any of the following cases, be solemnized on the authority of two certificates of a superintendent registrar.

(2) Case A is where—

   (a) the marriage is of a same sex couple according to the usages of the Society of Friends (commonly called Quakers), and

   (b) the relevant governing authority has given written consent to such marriages of same sex couples.

(3) For that purpose "relevant governing authority" means the recording clerk for the time being of the Society of Friends in London.

(4) Case B is where—

   (a) the marriage is of a same sex couple professing the Jewish religion according to the usages of the Jews, and

   (b) the relevant governing authority has given written consent to such marriages of same sex couples.

(5) For that purpose the meaning of "relevant governing authority" is to be determined in accordance with this table—

The "relevant governing authority" is... | ...if the marriage falls to be registered by... |

the Chief Rabbi of the United Hebrew Congregations of the Commonwealth | the secretary of a synagogue certified under paragraph (a) of the relevant definition (certification by the President of the Board of Deputies) |

the person or persons duly recognised by the members of—

   - the West London Synagogue of British Jews ("the West London Synagogue"), and

   - the other synagogues that are constituents of or affiliated to the Movement for Reform Judaism

— either the secretary of the West London Synagogue, as certified under paragraph (b) of the relevant definition

— or the secretary of another synagogue in a case where:

   - the secretary is certified under paragraph (d) of the relevant definition by the secretary of the West London Synagogue, and

- the synagogue is one of those which are constituents of or affiliated to the Movement for Reform Judaism
the person or persons duly recognised by the members of—
    - the Liberal Jewish Synagogue, St. John's Wood ("the St. John's Wood Synagogue"), and
    - the other synagogues that are constituents of or affiliated to Liberal Judaism
— either the secretary of the St. John's Wood Synagogue, as certified under paragraph (c) of the relevant definition
— or the secretary of another synagogue in a case where:
    - the secretary is certified under paragraph (d) of the relevant definition by the secretary of the St. John's Wood Synagogue, and
    - the synagogue is one of those which are constituents of or affiliated to Liberal Judaism
the secretary of a synagogue certified under paragraph (d) of the relevant definition (certification by the secretary of the West London Synagogue or the secretary of the St. John's Wood Synagogue) in a case where the synagogue is not one of those which are constituents of or affiliated to:
    - the Movement for Reform Judaism, or
    - Liberal Judaism
In that table—
    (a) "relevant definition" means the definition of "secretary of a synagogue" in section 67;
    (b) a reference to a person or persons being duly recognised is a reference to the person or persons being recognised for the purpose of giving consent for the purposes of this section.
(6) Case C is where—
    (a) the marriage is of a same sex couple according to religious rites or usages (other than the rites of the Church of England),
    (b) one or each of the couple is house-bound or a detained person,
    (c) the marriage is at the usual place of residence of the house-bound or detained person or persons, and
    (d) the relevant governing authority has given written consent to marriages of same sex couples according to those religious rites or usages.
(7) For that purpose—
"relevant governing authority" means the person or persons recognised by the members of the relevant religious organisation as competent for the purpose of giving consent for the purposes of this section;
"relevant religious organisation" means the religious organisation according to whose rites or usages the marriage is to be solemnized.
(8) Subsection (6) does not authorise a marriage that may be solemnized under subsection (2) or (4).".
Commencement Information
I6. S. 5 in force at 13.3.2014 by S.I. 2014/93, art. 3. (c)

Part 5 of the Marriage Act 1949.

6. Armed forces chapels

(1) Part 5 of the Marriage Act 1949 is amended as follows.
(2) Section 68 (solemnization of marriages in naval, military and air force chapels): after subsection (1) insert—
"(1. A)Nothing in this Part of this Act which applies to the marriage of same sex couples applies to marriage according to the rites of the Church of England.".
(3) Section 70 (registration of chapels for marriages otherwise than according to rites of Church of England): after subsection (3) insert—

"(4)This section does not apply to the marriage of same sex couples.".
(4) After section 70 insert—
"70. ARegistration of chapels for marriages of same sex couples otherwise than according to rites of Church of England
(1) The Secretary of State may apply to the Registrar General for a chapel to which this Part applies to be registered for the solemnization of marriages of same sex couples.
(2) Where an application is made under this section, subsections (1) to (3) of section 70 apply to the application as if it had been made under section 70.
(3) Where a chapel is registered on an application under this section, subsections (1) to (3) of section 70 apply in relation to the chapel as if it had been registered on an application under section 70.
(4) Any application for the cancellation of a registration is to be made by the Secretary of State.
(5) The Secretary of State may by statutory instrument make regulations about—
    (a) the registration of chapels under this section, and
    (b) the cancellation of registrations.
(6) The regulations may, in particular, make provision—
    (a) as to the procedures to be followed by the Secretary of State in making an application for registration or an application for cancellation of a registration;
    (b) as to the procedures to be followed by the Registrar General on an application for registration or an application for cancellation of a registration;
    (c) as to consents required before an application for registration may be made (including such provision amending section 2 of the Marriage (Same Sex Couples) Act 2013 as the Secretary of State considers appropriate to secure that the giving of such a consent is an opt-in activity under that section).
(7) A statutory instrument containing regulations under this section may not be made unless a draft of the instrument has been laid before, and approved by resolution of, each House of Parliament.
(8) In this section a reference to the cancellation of a registration is a reference to the cancellation, under section 70. (2) (as applied by this section), of a registration under this section.".
Commencement Information
I7. S. 6 in force at 21.1.2014 for specified purposes by S.I. 2014/93, art. 2. (a)
I8. S. 6 in force at 3.6.2014 in so far as not already in force by S.I. 2014/93, art. 5. (a)

The Marriage (Registrar General's Licence) Act 1970.

7. Opt-in: "deathbed marriages"

In section 1 of the Marriage (Registrar General's Licence) Act 1970 (marriages which may be solemnized by Registrar General's Licence), after subsection (2) insert—
"(3)A marriage of a same sex couple according to religious rites or usages may not be solemnized in accordance with this Act unless the relevant governing authority has given written consent to marriages of same sex couples according to those religious rites or usages.
(4) For that purpose—
"relevant governing authority" means the person or persons recognised by the members of the relevant religious organisation as competent for the purpose of giving consent for the purposes of this section;
"relevant religious organisation" means the religious organisation according to whose rites or usages the marriage is to be solemnized.".
Commencement Information
I9. S. 7 in force at 13.3.2014 by S.I. 2014/93, art. 3. (d)

The Church in Wales

8. Power to allow for marriage of same sex couples in Church in Wales

(1) This section applies if the Lord Chancellor is satisfied that the Governing Body of the Church in Wales has resolved that the law of England and Wales should be changed to allow for the marriage of same sex couples according to the rites of the Church in Wales.

(2) The Lord Chancellor must, by order, make such provision as the Lord Chancellor considers appropriate to allow for the marriage of same sex couples according to the rites of the Church in Wales.

(3) The provision that may be made by an order under this section includes provision amending England and Wales legislation.

(4) In making an order under this section, the Lord Chancellor must have regard to the terms of the resolution of the Governing Body mentioned in subsection (1).

(5) If it appears to the Lord Chancellor—

   (a) that a reference in this section to the Governing Body has ceased to be appropriate by reason of a change in the governance arrangements of the Church in Wales, the reference has effect as a reference to such person or persons as the Lord Chancellor thinks appropriate; or

   (b) that a reference in this section to a resolution has ceased to be appropriate for that reason, the reference has effect as a reference to such decision or decisions as the Lord Chancellor thinks appropriate.

(6) In Schedule 7 to the Constitutional Reform Act 2005 (functions of the Lord Chancellor which may not be transferred under the Ministers of the Crown Act 1975), in paragraph 4, at the end of Part A insert—

Section 8".

Commencement Information

I10. S. 8 in force at 13.3.2014 by S.I. 2014/93, art. 3. (d)

Other provisions relating to marriages of same sex couples

9. Conversion of civil partnership into marriage

(1) The parties to an England and Wales civil partnership may convert their civil partnership into a marriage under a procedure established by regulations made by the Secretary of State.

(2) The parties to a civil partnership within subsection (3) may convert their civil partnership into a marriage under a procedure established by regulations made by the Secretary of State.

(3) A civil partnership is within this subsection if—

   (a) it was formed outside the United Kingdom under an Order in Council made under Chapter 1 of Part 5 of the Civil Partnership Act 2004 (registration at British consulates etc or by armed forces personnel), and

   (b) the part of the United Kingdom that was relevant for the purposes of section 210. (2)(b) or (as the case may be) section 211. (2)(b) of that Act was England and Wales.

(4) Regulations under this section may in particular make—

   (a) provision about the making by the parties to a civil partnership of an application to convert their civil partnership into a marriage;

   (b) provision about the information to be provided in support of an application to convert;

   (c) provision about the making of declarations in support of an application to convert;

   (d) provision for persons who have made an application to convert to appear before any person or attend at any place;

(e) provision conferring functions in connection with applications to convert on relevant officials, relevant armed forces personnel, the Secretary of State, or any other persons;

(f) provision for fees, of such amounts as are specified in or determined in accordance with the regulations, to be payable in respect of—

(i) the making of an application to convert;

(ii) the exercise of any function conferred by virtue of paragraph (e).

(5) Functions conferred by virtue of paragraph (e) of subsection (4) may include functions relating to—

(a) the recording of information on the conversion of civil partnerships;

(b) the issuing of certified copies of any information recorded;

[F1. (ba)the carrying out, on request, of searches of any information recorded and the provision, on request, of records of any information recorded (otherwise than in the form of certified copies);]

(c) the conducting of services or ceremonies (other than religious services or ceremonies) following the conversion of a civil partnership.

[F2. (5. A)Subsection (5. B) applies where regulations under this section provide for a fee to be payable to a superintendent registrar or registrar.

(5. B)The regulations may provide for such part of the fee as may be specified in or determined in accordance with the regulations to be payable by the superintendent registrar or registrar to the Registrar General in such circumstances as may be set out in the regulations.

(5. C)The regulations may provide for the reduction, waiver or refund of part or all of a fee whether by conferring a discretion or otherwise.]

(6)Where a civil partnership is converted into a marriage under this section—

(a) the civil partnership ends on the conversion, and

(b) the resulting marriage is to be treated as having subsisted since the date the civil partnership was formed.

(7)In this section—

" England and Wales civil partnership " means a civil partnership which is formed by two people registering as civil partners of each other in England or Wales (see Part 2 of the Civil Partnership Act 2004);

" relevant armed forces personnel " means—

- a member of Her Majesty's forces;

- a civilian subject to service discipline (within the meaning of the Armed Forces Act 2006);

and for this purpose " Her Majesty's forces " has the same meaning as in the Armed Forces Act 2006;

" relevant official " means—

- the Registrar General;

- a superintendent registrar;

- a registrar;

- a consular officer in the service of Her Majesty's government in the United Kingdom;

- a person authorised by the Secretary of State in respect of the solemnization of marriages or formation of civil partnerships in a country or territory in which Her Majesty's government in the United Kingdom has for the time being no consular representative.

Amendments (Textual)

F1 S. 9. (5)(ba) inserted (26.5.2015) by Deregulation Act 2015 (c. 20) , ss. 99. (3) , 115. (3)(k)

F2 S. 9. (5. A)-(5. C) inserted (12.7.2016) by Immigration Act 2016 (c. 19) , s. 94. (1) , Sch. 15 para. 5 ; S.I. 2016/603 , reg. 3. (w)

Commencement Information

I11 S. 9. (1)-(5) (7) in force at 30.6.2014 for specified purposes by S.I. 2014/1662 , art. 2. (a)

I12 S. 9. (1)-(5) (7) in force at 10.12.2014 in so far as not already in force by S.I. 2014/3169 , art. 2

I13 S. 9. (6) in force at 10.12.2014 by S.I. 2014/3169 , art. 2

10. Extra-territorial matters

(1) A marriage under—
    (a) the law of any part of the United Kingdom (other than England and Wales), or
    (b) the law of any country or territory outside the United Kingdom,
is not prevented from being recognised under the law of England and Wales only because it is the marriage of a same sex couple.
(2) For the purposes of this section it is irrelevant whether the law of a particular part of the United Kingdom, or a particular country or territory outside the United Kingdom—
    (a) already provides for marriage of same sex couples at the time when this section comes into force, or
    (b) provides for marriage of same sex couples from a later time.
(3) Schedule 2 (extra-territorial matters) has effect.
Commencement Information
I14. S. 10. (1)(2) in force at 13.3.2014 by S.I. 2014/93, art. 3. (e) (with art. 4)
I15. S. 10. (3) in force at 31.10.2013 for specified purposes by S.I. 2013/2789, art. 3. (d)
I16. S. 10. (3) in force at 13.3.2014 for specified purposes by S.I. 2014/93, art. 3. (h)

Effect of extension of marriage

11. Effect of extension of marriage

(1) In the law of England and Wales, marriage has the same effect in relation to same sex couples as it has in relation to opposite sex couples.
(2) The law of England and Wales (including all England and Wales legislation whenever passed or made) has effect in accordance with subsection (1).
(3) Schedule 3 (interpretation of legislation) has effect.
(4) Schedule 4 (effect of extension of marriage: further provision) has effect.
(5) For provision about limitations on the effects of subsections (1) and (2) and Schedule 3, see Part 7 of Schedule 4.
(6) Subsections (1) and (2) and Schedule 3 do not have any effect in relation to—
    (a) Measures and Canons of the Church of England (whenever passed or made),
    (b) subordinate legislation (whenever made) made under a Measure or Canon of the Church of England, or
    (c) other ecclesiastical law (whether or not contained in England and Wales legislation, and, if contained in England and Wales legislation, whenever passed or made).
(7) In Schedules 3 and 4—
"existing England and Wales legislation" means—
    - in the case of England and Wales legislation that is primary legislation, legislation passed before the end of the Session in which this Act is passed (excluding this Act), or
    - in the case of England and Wales legislation that is subordinate legislation, legislation made on or before the day on which this Act is passed (excluding legislation made under this Act);
"new England and Wales legislation" means—
    - in the case of England and Wales legislation that is primary legislation, legislation passed after the end of the Session in which this Act is passed, or
    - in the case of England and Wales legislation that is subordinate legislation, legislation made after the day on which this Act is passed.
Modifications etc. (not altering text)
C1. S. 11. (1)(2) excluded (13.3.2014) by The Marriage (Same Sex Couples) Act 2013

(Consequential and Contrary Provisions and Scotland) Order 2014 (S.I. 2014/560), art. 1. (2), Sch. 2 para. 2

C2. S. 11. (1)(2) modified by SI 2010/990, regs. 2. A(5), 2. B(5) (as inserted (13.3.2014) by The Marriage (Same Sex Couples) Act 2013 (Consequential and Contrary Provisions and Scotland) Order 2014 (S.I. 2014/560), art. 1. (2), Sch. 3 para. 17)

C3. S. 11. (1)(2) modified by SI 1992/129, Sch. 2 Scheme, Sch. 1 Pt. 3, rules 1. (5), 2. (5) (as inserted (13.3.2014) by The Marriage (Same Sex Couples) Act 2013 (Consequential and Contrary Provisions and Scotland) Order 2014 (S.I. 2014/560), art. 1. (2), Sch. 3 para. 17)

C4. S. 11. (1)(2) excluded (13.3.2014) by The Marriage (Same Sex Couples) Act 2013 (Consequential and Contrary Provisions and Scotland) Order 2014 (S.I. 2014/560), art. 1. (2), Sch. 2 para. 1

C5. S. 11. (1)(2) modified (13.3.2014) by The Marriage (Same Sex Couples) Act 2013 (Consequential and Contrary Provisions and Scotland) Order 2014 (S.I. 2014/560), art. 1. (2), Sch. 2 para. 4

C6. S. 11. (1)(2) excluded (13.3.2014) by The Marriage (Same Sex Couples) Act 2013 (Consequential and Contrary Provisions and Scotland) Order 2014 (S.I. 2014/560), art. 1. (2), Sch. 2 para. 3

C7. S. 11. (1)(2) modified by SI 1992/1612, regs. 42. B(5), 42. C(5) (as inserted (13.3.2014) by The Marriage (Same Sex Couples) Act 2013 (Consequential and Contrary Provisions and Scotland) Order 2014 (S.I. 2014/560), art. 1. (2), Sch. 3 para. 17)

C8. S. 11. (1)(2) modified by SI 2006/3432, rules 4. (4), 5. (5) (as inserted (13.3.2014) by The Marriage (Same Sex Couples) Act 2013 (Consequential and Contrary Provisions and Scotland) Order 2014 (S.I. 2014/560), art. 1. (2), Sch. 3 para. 17)

C9. S. 11. (1)(2) excluded (13.3.2014) by The Marriage (Same Sex Couples) Act 2013 (Consequential and Contrary Provisions and Scotland) Order 2014 (S.I. 2014/560), art. 1. (2), Sch. 2 para. 5

C10. S. 11. (1)(2) modified by SI 2012/687, rules 2. A(5), 2. B(5) (as inserted (13.3.2014) by The Marriage (Same Sex Couples) Act 2013 (Consequential and Contrary Provisions and Scotland) Order 2014 (S.I. 2014/560), art. 1. (2), Sch. 3 para. 17)

Commencement Information

I17. S. 11. (1)-(3)(5)-(7) in force at 13.3.2014 by S.I. 2014/93, art. 3. (f)

I18. S. 11. (4) in force at 31.10.2013 for specified purposes by S.I. 2013/2789, art. 3. (e)

I19. S. 11. (4) in force at 31.10.2013 for specified purposes by S.I. 2013/2789, art. 2. (b)

I20. S. 11. (4) in force at 13.3.2014 for specified purposes by S.I. 2014/93, art. 3. (j)

I21. S. 11. (4) in force at 30.6.2014 for specified purposes by S.I. 2014/1662, art. 3. (c)

I22. S. 11. (4) in force at 10.12.2014 for specified purposes by S.I. 2014/3169, art. 2

Part 3. of the Marriage Act 1949

3. Marriage for which no opt-in necessary

In Part 3 of the Marriage Act 1949, for section 26 substitute—

"26. Marriage of a man and a woman; marriage of same sex couples for which no opt-in necessary

(1) The following marriages may be solemnized on the authority of two certificates of a superintendent registrar—

"(a)a marriage of a man and a woman, in a building registered under section 41, according to such form and ceremony as the persons to be married see fit to adopt;

(b) a marriage of any couple in the office of a superintendent registrar;

(bb) a marriage of any couple on approved premises;

(c) a marriage of a man and a woman according to the usages of the Society of Friends

14

(commonly called Quakers);

(d) a marriage between a man and a woman professing the Jewish religion according to the usages of the Jews;

(dd) a qualifying residential marriage;

(e) a marriage of a man and a woman according to the rites of the Church of England in any church or chapel in which banns of matrimony may be published."

(2) In this section "qualifying residential marriage" means—

(a) the marriage of a man and a woman (other than a marriage in pursuance of subsection (1)(c) or (d) above), one or each of whom is house-bound or a detained person, at the usual place of residence of the house-bound or detained person or persons, or

(b) the marriage of a same sex couple (other than a marriage according to the rites of the Church of England or other religious rites or usages), one or each of whom is house-bound or a detained person, at the usual place of residence of the house-bound or detained person or persons.".

Commencement Information

I1. S. 3 in force at 13.3.2014 by S.I. 2014/93, art. 3. (a)

4. Opt-in: marriage in places of worship

(1) After section 26 of the Marriage Act 1949 insert—

"26. AOpt-in to marriage of same sex couples: places of worship

(1) A marriage of a same sex couple in an appropriately registered building according to such form and ceremony as the persons to be married see fit to adopt may be solemnized on the authority of two certificates of a superintendent registrar.

(2) For the purposes of this section "appropriately registered building" means a building which has been registered under section 43. A.

(3) An application for registration of a building under section 43. A may not be made unless the relevant governing authority has given written consent to marriages of same sex couples.

(4) For that purpose, in relation to a building—

"relevant governing authority" means the person or persons recognised by the members of the relevant religious organisation as competent for the purpose of giving consent for the purposes of this section;

"relevant religious organisation" means the religious organisation for whose religious purposes the building is used.

(5) Nothing in this section is to be taken to relate or have any reference to marriages solemnized according to the rites of the Church of England.

(6) This section is subject (in particular) to sections 44. A to 44. C (registration of shared buildings for marriage of same sex couples) and regulations made under any of those sections.".

(2) Schedule 1 (registration of buildings etc) has effect.

Commencement Information

I2. S. 4 in force at 31.10.2013 for specified purposes by S.I. 2013/2789, art. 2. (a)

I3. S. 4 in force at 13.3.2014 in so far as not already in force by S.I. 2014/93, art. 3. (b)

5. Opt-in: other religious ceremonies

After section 26. A of the Marriage Act 1949 insert—

"26. BOpt-in to marriage of same sex couples: other religious ceremonies

(1) A marriage may, in any of the following cases, be solemnized on the authority of two certificates of a superintendent registrar.

(2) Case A is where—

(a) the marriage is of a same sex couple according to the usages of the Society of Friends (commonly called Quakers), and

(b) the relevant governing authority has given written consent to such marriages of same sex couples.

(3) For that purpose "relevant governing authority" means the recording clerk for the time being of the Society of Friends in London.

(4) Case B is where—

(a) the marriage is of a same sex couple professing the Jewish religion according to the usages of the Jews, and

(b) the relevant governing authority has given written consent to such marriages of same sex couples.

(5) For that purpose the meaning of "relevant governing authority" is to be determined in accordance with this table—

The "relevant governing authority" is... | ...if the marriage falls to be registered by... |

the Chief Rabbi of the United Hebrew Congregations of the Commonwealth | the secretary of a synagogue certified under paragraph (a) of the relevant definition (certification by the President of the Board of Deputies) |

the person or persons duly recognised by the members of—

- the West London Synagogue of British Jews ("the West London Synagogue"), and

- the other synagogues that are constituents of or affiliated to the Movement for Reform Judaism

— either the secretary of the West London Synagogue, as certified under paragraph (b) of the relevant definition

— or the secretary of another synagogue in a case where:

- the secretary is certified under paragraph (d) of the relevant definition by the secretary of the West London Synagogue, and

- the synagogue is one of those which are constituents of or affiliated to the Movement for Reform Judaism

the person or persons duly recognised by the members of—

- the Liberal Jewish Synagogue, St. John's Wood ("the St. John's Wood Synagogue"), and

- the other synagogues that are constituents of or affiliated to Liberal Judaism

— either the secretary of the St. John's Wood Synagogue, as certified under paragraph (c) of the relevant definition

— or the secretary of another synagogue in a case where:

- the secretary is certified under paragraph (d) of the relevant definition by the secretary of the St. John's Wood Synagogue, and

- the synagogue is one of those which are constituents of or affiliated to Liberal Judaism

the secretary of a synagogue certified under paragraph (d) of the relevant definition (certification by the secretary of the West London Synagogue or the secretary of the St. John's Wood Synagogue) in a case where the synagogue is not one of those which are constituents of or affiliated to:

- the Movement for Reform Judaism, or

- Liberal Judaism

In that table—

(a) "relevant definition" means the definition of "secretary of a synagogue" in section 67;

(b) a reference to a person or persons being duly recognised is a reference to the person or persons being recognised for the purpose of giving consent for the purposes of this section.

(6) Case C is where—

(a) the marriage is of a same sex couple according to religious rites or usages (other than the rites of the Church of England),

(b) one or each of the couple is house-bound or a detained person,

(c) the marriage is at the usual place of residence of the house-bound or detained person or persons, and

(d) the relevant governing authority has given written consent to marriages of same sex couples according to those religious rites or usages.

(7) For that purpose—

"relevant governing authority" means the person or persons recognised by the members of the relevant religious organisation as competent for the purpose of giving consent for the purposes of this section;

"relevant religious organisation" means the religious organisation according to whose rites or usages the marriage is to be solemnized.

(8) Subsection (6) does not authorise a marriage that may be solemnized under subsection (2) or (4).".

Commencement Information

I4. S. 5 in force at 13.3.2014 by S.I. 2014/93, art. 3. (c)

Part 5. of the Marriage Act 1949

6. Armed forces chapels

(1) Part 5 of the Marriage Act 1949 is amended as follows.

(2) Section 68 (solemnization of marriages in naval, military and air force chapels): after subsection (1) insert—

"(1. A)Nothing in this Part of this Act which applies to the marriage of same sex couples applies to marriage according to the rites of the Church of England.".

(3) Section 70 (registration of chapels for marriages otherwise than according to rites of Church of England): after subsection (3) insert—

"(4)This section does not apply to the marriage of same sex couples.".

(4) After section 70 insert—

"70. ARegistration of chapels for marriages of same sex couples otherwise than according to rites of Church of England

(1) The Secretary of State may apply to the Registrar General for a chapel to which this Part applies to be registered for the solemnization of marriages of same sex couples.

(2) Where an application is made under this section, subsections (1) to (3) of section 70 apply to the application as if it had been made under section 70.

(3) Where a chapel is registered on an application under this section, subsections (1) to (3) of section 70 apply in relation to the chapel as if it had been registered on an application under section 70.

(4) Any application for the cancellation of a registration is to be made by the Secretary of State.

(5) The Secretary of State may by statutory instrument make regulations about—

    (a) the registration of chapels under this section, and

    (b) the cancellation of registrations.

(6) The regulations may, in particular, make provision—

    (a) as to the procedures to be followed by the Secretary of State in making an application for registration or an application for cancellation of a registration;

    (b) as to the procedures to be followed by the Registrar General on an application for registration or an application for cancellation of a registration;

    (c) as to consents required before an application for registration may be made (including such provision amending section 2 of the Marriage (Same Sex Couples) Act 2013 as the Secretary of State considers appropriate to secure that the giving of such a consent is an opt-in activity under that section).

(7) A statutory instrument containing regulations under this section may not be made unless a draft of the instrument has been laid before, and approved by resolution of, each House of Parliament.

(8) In this section a reference to the cancellation of a registration is a reference to the cancellation, under section 70. (2) (as applied by this section), of a registration under this section.".

Commencement Information

I1. S. 6 in force at 21.1.2014 for specified purposes by S.I. 2014/93, art. 2. (a)
I2. S. 6 in force at 3.6.2014 in so far as not already in force by S.I. 2014/93, art. 5. (a)

PART 2. Other provisions relating to marriage and civil partnership

PART 2 Other provisions relating to marriage and civil partnership

12. Change of gender of married persons or civil partners

Schedule 5 (change of gender of married persons or civil partners) has effect.
Commencement Information
I1. S. 12 in force at 30.6.2014 for specified purposes by S.I. 2014/1662, art. 2. (b)
I2. S. 12 in force at 10.12.2014 in so far as not already in force by S.I. 2014/3169, art. 2

13. Marriage overseas

(1) Schedule 6 (marriage overseas) has effect.
(2) The Foreign Marriage Act 1892 is repealed.
Commencement Information
I3. S. 13. (1) in force at 21.1.2014 for specified purposes by S.I. 2014/93, art. 2. (b)
I4. S. 13. (1) in force at 3.6.2014 in so far as not already in force by S.I. 2014/93, art. 5. (b)
I5. S. 13. (2) in force at 3.6.2014 by S.I. 2014/93, art. 5. (b)

14. Marriage according to the usages of belief organisations

(1) The Secretary of State must arrange for a review of—
    (a) whether an order under subsection (4) should be made permitting marriages according to the usages of belief organisations to be solemnized on the authority of certificates of a superintendent registrar, and
    (b) if so, what provision should be included in the order.
(2) The arrangements made by the Secretary of State under subsection (1) must provide for the review to include a full public consultation.
(3) The Secretary of State must arrange for a report on the outcome of the review to be produced and published before 1 January 2015.
(4) The Secretary of State may by order make provision for and in connection with permitting marriages according to the usages of belief organisations to be solemnized on the authority of certificates of a superintendent registrar.
(5) An order under subsection (4) may—
    (a) amend any England and Wales legislation;
    (b) make provision for the charging of fees.
(6) An order under subsection (4) must provide that no religious service may be used at a marriage which is solemnized in pursuance of the order.
(7) In this section "belief organisation" means an organisation whose principal or sole purpose is the advancement of a system of non-religious beliefs which relate to morality or ethics.
Commencement Information

16. S. 14 in force at 31.10.2013 by S.I. 2013/2789, art. 3. (a)

15. Review of civil partnership

(1) The Secretary of State must arrange—
 (a) for the operation and future of the Civil Partnership Act 2004 in England and Wales to be reviewed, and
 (b) for a report on the outcome of the review to be produced and published.
(2) Subsection (1) does not prevent the review from also dealing with other matters relating to civil partnership.
(3) The arrangements made by the Secretary of State must provide for the review to begin as soon as practicable and include a full public consultation.

16. Survivor benefits under occupational pension schemes

(1) The Secretary of State must arrange for a review of the following matters relating to occupational pension schemes—
 (a) relevant differences in survivor benefits;
 (b) the costs, and other effects, of securing that relevant differences in survivor benefits are eliminated by the equalisation of survivor benefits.
(2) For the purposes of this section, each of the following are relevant differences in survivor benefits—
 (a) differences between—
(i) same sex survivor benefits, and
(ii) opposite sex survivor benefits provided to widows;
 (b) differences between—
(i) same sex survivor benefits, and
(ii) opposite sex survivor benefits provided to widowers;
 (c) differences between—
(i) opposite sex survivor benefits provided to widows, and
(ii) opposite sex survivor benefits provided to widowers.
(3) The review must, in particular, consider these issues—
 (a) the extent to which same sex survivor benefits are provided in reliance on paragraph 18 of Schedule 9 to the Equality Act 2010;
 (b) the extent to which—
(i) same sex survivor benefits, and
(ii) opposite sex survivor benefits,
are calculated by reference to different periods of pensionable service.
(4) The arrangements made by the Secretary of State must provide for the person or persons conducting the review to consult such other persons as the Secretary of State considers appropriate.
(5) The Secretary of State must arrange for a report on the outcome of the review to be produced and published before 1 July 2014.
(6) If the Secretary of State, having considered the outcome of the review, thinks that the law of England and Wales and Scotland should be changed for the purpose of eliminating or reducing relevant differences in survivor benefits, the Secretary of State may, by order, make such provision as the Secretary of State considers appropriate for that purpose.
(7) An order under subsection (6) may amend—
 (a) England and Wales legislation;
 (b) Scottish legislation.
(8) In this section—
"occupational pension scheme" has the same meaning as in the Pension Schemes Act 1993 (see

section 1 of that Act);

"opposite sex survivor benefits" means survivor benefits provided to surviving spouses of marriages of opposite sex couples;

"same sex survivor benefits" means survivor benefits provided to—

    - surviving civil partners, and

    - surviving spouses of marriages of same sex couples;

"survivor benefits" means survivor benefits provided under occupational pension schemes.

PART 3. Final provisions

PART 3 Final provisions

17. Transitional and consequential provision

(1) The Secretary of State or Lord Chancellor may, by order, make such transitional, transitory or saving provision as the Secretary of State or Lord Chancellor considers appropriate in connection with the coming into force of any provision of this Act.

(2) The Secretary of State or Lord Chancellor may, by order, make such provision as the Secretary of State or Lord Chancellor considers appropriate in consequence of this Act.

(3) The provision that may be made by an order under subsection (1) or (2) includes provision amending UK legislation.

(4) Schedule 7 (transitional and consequential provision etc) has effect.

Commencement Information

I1. S. 17. (1)-(3) in force at 31.10.2013 by S.I. 2013/2789, art. 3. (b)

I2. S. 17. (4) in force at 13.3.2014 for specified purposes by S.I. 2014/93, art. 3. (k)

I3. S. 17. (4) in force at 3.6.2014 for specified purposes by S.I. 2014/93, art. 5. (d)

I4. S. 17. (4) in force at 10.12.2014 in so far as not already in force by S.I. 2014/3169, art. 2

18. Orders and regulations

(1) Any power of the Secretary of State or Lord Chancellor to make an order or regulations under this Act is exercisable by statutory instrument.

(2) The following subordinate legislation may not be made by the Secretary of State or Lord Chancellor unless a draft of the statutory instrument containing the legislation has been laid before, and approved by resolution of, each House of Parliament—

    (a) an order under section 8;

    (b) the first regulations under section 9. (1);

    (c) the first regulations under section 9. (2);

    (d) an order under section 14;

    (e) an order under section 16;

    (f) an order under section 17. (1) or (2) which amends an Act of Parliament;

    (g) an order under paragraph 1 of Schedule 2;

    (h) an order under paragraph 2 of Schedule 2;

    (i) an order under paragraph 27 of Schedule 4;

    (j) an order under paragraph 9. (8) of Schedule 6.

(3) The following subordinate legislation made by the Secretary of State or Lord Chancellor is subject to annulment in pursuance of a resolution of either House of Parliament—

    (a) regulations under section 9. (1) (except for the first such regulations);

    (b) regulations under section 9. (2) (except for the first such regulations);

(c) an order under section 17. (1) or (2) (unless it amends an Act of Parliament).

(4) An order or regulations made under this Act may—

    (a) make different provision for different purposes,

    (b) make transitional, transitory or saving provision, or

    (c) make consequential provision.

(5) The provision that the Secretary of State may make in any relevant instrument includes provision enabling the Registrar General to make regulations by statutory instrument (with or without the consent of a minister of the Crown).

(6) But the Secretary of State—

    (a) may not make enabling provision which gives the Registrar General power to require a fee to be paid or power to set the amount of a fee; and

    (b) may not make other enabling provision unless the Secretary of State is satisfied that the provision is necessary in connection with administrative matters relating to functions of the Registrar General or functions of superintendent registrars or registrars.

(7) Regulations made by the Registrar General under any enabling provision are subject to annulment in pursuance of a resolution of either House of Parliament.

(8) But that is subject to any provision in a relevant instrument about the kind of Parliamentary scrutiny, if any, to which the regulations are to be subject.

(9) In subsections (5) to (8)—

"enabling provision" means provision made under subsection (5) enabling the Registrar General to make regulations;

"relevant instrument" means—

    - regulations under section 9. (1) or (2), or

    - an order under section 14. (4).

(10) Any power of the Secretary of State or Lord Chancellor under this Act to amend legislation by subordinate legislation includes power to repeal or revoke legislation (and any reference to the amendment of legislation by such an order or regulations is to be read accordingly).

(11) The Secretary of State or Lord Chancellor must—

    (a) obtain the consent of the Scottish Ministers before making any order or regulations under this Act, except an order under section 21. (3), containing provision which would (if contained in an Act of the Scottish Parliament) be within the legislative competence of that Parliament;

    (b) obtain the consent of the Department of Finance and Personnel before making any order or regulations under this Act, except an order under section 21. (3), containing provision which would (if contained in an Act of the Northern Ireland Assembly) be within the legislative competence of that Assembly.

Commencement Information

I5. S. 18 in force at 31.10.2013 by S.I. 2013/2789, art. 3. (c)

19. Interpretation

(1) In this Act, an expression set out in an entry in the first column of this table has the meaning given in the corresponding entry in the second column.

Expression | Meaning |

— an Act of Parliament

— an Act of the National Assembly for Wales

— a Measure of the National Assembly for Wales

— an Act of the Scottish Parliament

— an Act of the Northern Ireland Assembly

— a Measure of the Church of England

— a Canon of the Church of England

— any Order in Council, order, rules, regulations, schemes, warrants, byelaws and other instruments made under primary legislation or under a Canon of the Church of England

England and Wales legislation | primary legislation and subordinate legislation which forms part of the law of England and Wales (whether or not it also forms part of the law of another jurisdiction) |
Northern Ireland legislation | primary legislation and subordinate legislation which forms part of the law of Northern Ireland (whether or not it also forms part of the law of another jurisdiction) |
Scottish legislation | primary legislation and subordinate legislation which forms part of the law of Scotland (whether or not it also forms part of the law of another jurisdiction) |
— England and Wales legislation
— Scottish legislation
— Northern Ireland legislation
(2) In this Act—
"existing England and Wales legislation" has the meaning given in section 11;
"new England and Wales legislation" has the meaning given in section 11;
"registrar" means a registrar of births, deaths and marriages;
"Registrar General" means the Registrar General of England and Wales;
"superintendent registrar" means a superintendent registrar of births, deaths and marriages.
(3) For further interpretation provision relating to this Act, see paragraph 5 of Schedule 3.
Commencement Information
I6. S. 19 in force at 31.10.2013 by S.I. 2013/2789, art. 3. (c)

20. Extent

(1) This Act extends to England and Wales.
(2) These provisions of this Act also extend to Scotland—
    (a) in Part 1, section 10. (3) and Schedule 2;
    (b) Part 2, except for sections 14 and 15;
    (c) Part 3.
(3) These provisions of this Act also extend to Northern Ireland—
    (a) in Part 1, section 10. (3) and Schedule 2;
    (b) Part 2, except for sections 14 to 16 and paragraphs 4, 5, 10 and 11 of Schedule 6;
    (c) Part 3.
(4) Subsections (1) to (3) do not apply to an amendment or repeal or revocation made by this Act.
(5) An amendment or repeal or revocation made by this Act has the same extent as the provision amended or repealed or revoked.
(6) Subsection (5) is subject to subsections (7) to (9).
(7) Any amendment of the following Acts extends to England and Wales only—
    (a) the Social Security Contributions and Benefits Act 1992;
    (b) the Pension Schemes Act 1993;
    (c) the Human Fertilisation and Embryology Act 2008.
(8) The repeal of the Foreign Marriage Act 1892 made by section 13. (2) does not extend to Northern Ireland.
(9) Any amendment made by Part 2 of Schedule 5 does not extend to Northern Ireland.
Commencement Information
I7. S. 20 in force at 31.10.2013 by S.I. 2013/2789, art. 3. (c)

21. Short title and commencement

(1) This Act may be cited as the Marriage (Same Sex Couples) Act 2013.
(2) This section and sections 15 and 16 come into force on the day on which this Act is passed.
(3) Subject to that, this Act comes into force on such day as the Secretary of State may by order appoint; and different days may be appointed for different purposes.

Schedules

Schedule 1. Registration of buildings etc

Section 4

Introduction

1. Part 3 of the Marriage Act 1949 is amended in accordance with this Schedule.
Commencement Information
I1. Sch. 1 para. 1 in force at 31.10.2013 for specified purposes by S.I. 2013/2789, art. 2. (a)
I2. Sch. 1 para. 1 in force at 13.3.2014 in so far as not already in force by S.I. 2014/93, art. 3. (g)

Registration of buildings

2. After section 43 insert—

"43. ARegistration of buildings: marriage of same sex couples

(1) A building that has been certified as required by law as a place of religious worship may be registered under this section for the solemnization of marriages of same sex couples.
(2) Any application for registration of a building under this section is to be made—
(a) by a proprietor or trustee of the building;
(b) to the superintendent registrar of the registration district in which the building is situated.
(3) An application for registration of a building under this section must be accompanied by—
(a) a certificate, given by the applicant and dated not earlier than one month before the making of the application, that the persons who are the relevant governing authority in relation to the building have given written consent to marriages of same sex couples as mentioned in section 26. A(3),
(b) a copy of that consent, and
(c) if the building is not already registered under section 41, a certificate of use for religious worship.
(4) The superintendent registrar must send to the Registrar General—
(a) the certificate or certificates, and
(b) the copy of the consent,
which accompany an application under this section.
(5) The Registrar General must then register the building.
(6) A building may be registered for the solemnization of marriages under this section whether it is a separate building or forms part of another building.
(7) In this section, in relation to an application under this section, "certificate of use for religious worship" means a certificate given by at least twenty householders and dated not earlier than one month before the making of the application, stating that they—
(a) use the building as their usual place of public religious worship, and
(b) wish the building to be registered under this section.

43. BBuildings registered under section 43. A: appointment of authorised persons

(1) For the purpose of enabling marriages to be solemnized in a building registered under section 43. A without the presence of a registrar, the trustees or governing body of that building may authorise a person to be present at the solemnization of marriages in that building.

(2) Where a person is so authorised in respect of any building registered under section 43. A, the trustees or governing body of that building must certify the name and address of the person so authorised to—

    (a) the Registrar General, and

    (b) the superintendent registrar of the registration district in which the building is situated.

(3) The power conferred by this section may only be exercised after the end of the relevant one year period (and, if that period has ended before the date of the registration under section 43. A, the power may accordingly be exercised immediately).

(4) The relevant one year period is the period of one year beginning with the date of the registration of the building under section 43. A (the "new registration").

(5) But if—

    (a) there is any earlier registration of the building under section 41 which is still in force at the date of the new registration, or

    (b) there has been any earlier qualifying registration of a previous building,

the relevant one year period is the period of one year beginning with the date of that registration (or the earlier of those dates).

(6) For that purpose there is a qualifying registration of a previous building if—

    (a) the congregation on whose behalf the new registration is made previously used another building for the purpose of public religious worship,

    (b) that building was registered under section 41 or 43. A, and

    (c) that registration was cancelled not more than one month before the date of the new registration.

(7) A reference in this section to the solemnization of marriage is a reference to the solemnization of marriage of a same sex couple.

(8) Nothing in this section is to be taken to relate or have any reference to marriages solemnized according to the usages of the Society of Friends or of persons professing the Jewish religion.

43. CCancellation of registration under section 43. A

(1) The registration of a building under section 43. A may be cancelled under this section.

(2) Any application under this section is to be made—

    (a) by a proprietor or trustee of the building;

    (b) to the superintendent registrar of the registration district in which the building is situated.

(3) The superintendent registrar must forward any application under this section to the Registrar General; and the Registrar General must then cancel the registration of the building.

(4) This section is subject (in particular) to sections 44. A to 44. C (registration of shared buildings for marriage of same sex couples) and regulations made under any of those sections.

43. DRegulations about sections 41 and 43 and 43. A to 43. C

(1) The Secretary of State may by statutory instrument make regulations about the procedures to be followed and the fees payable—

    (a) on registration applications;

    (b) in relation to section 43. B authorisations;

    (c) on cancellation applications.

(2) The Secretary of State may by statutory instrument make—

    (a) regulations modifying the application of section 41 or 43 in relation to buildings that are already registered under section 43. A;

(b) regulations about cases where a person makes applications under sections 41 and 43. A, or gives or certifies authorisations under sections 43 and 43. B, in respect of the same building at the same time (including provision modifying any requirement imposed by any of those sections or by regulations under subsection (1) of this section).

(3) A statutory instrument containing regulations made under this section is subject to annulment in pursuance of a resolution of either House of Parliament.

(4) In this section—

"cancellation application" means an application under section 43. C for the cancellation of the registration of a building;

"registration application" means an application under section 43. A for the registration of a building;

"section 43. B authorisation" means the authorisation of a person under section 43. B to be present at the solemnization of marriages in a building registered under section 43. A.".

Commencement Information

I3. Sch. 1 para. 2 in force at 31.10.2013 for specified purposes by S.I. 2013/2789, art. 2. (a)

I4. Sch. 1 para. 2 in force at 13.3.2014 in so far as not already in force by S.I. 2014/93, art. 3. (g)

Shared buildings

3. After section 44 insert—

44. ABuilding subject to Sharing of Church Buildings Act 1969: registration

(1) This section applies to a registration application relating to a building that is—

    (a) subject to a sharing agreement, or

    (b) used as mentioned in section 6. (4) of the 1969 Act.

(2) The registration application must be made in accordance with section 43. A (as read with section 26. A(3)).

(3) But those provisions have effect subject to the following provisions of this section.

(4) Each of the sharing churches is a relevant religious organisation for the purposes of section 26. A(3).

(5) A consent given under section 26. A(3) (a "consent to marriages of same sex couples") by the relevant governing authority of any of the sharing churches is therefore sufficient for the registration application to be made in compliance with section 26. A(3) (and references to the consent of the relevant governing authority in section 43. A are to be read accordingly).

(6) But the registration application may not be made unless the relevant governing authorities of each of the sharing churches (other than those which have given consents to marriages of same sex couples) have given a separate written consent to the use of the shared building for the solemnization of marriages of same sex couples (a "consent to use").

(7) The registration application must also be accompanied by—

    (a) a certificate, given by the applicant and dated not more than one month before the making of the application, that the relevant governing authorities mentioned in subsection (6) have given written consents to use, and

    (b) copies of those consents.

(8) The superintendent registrar must also send to the Registrar General—

    (a) the certificate, and

    (b) the copies of the consents,

which accompany the application in accordance with subsection (7).

(9) The Registrar General must not register the shared building unless and until subsection (8) and the requirements of section 43. A have been complied with.

(10) The Secretary of State may by statutory instrument make regulations containing such provision supplementing this section as the Secretary of State thinks appropriate.

44. BBuilding subject to Sharing of Church Buildings Act 1969: cancellation

(1) This section applies to a cancellation application relating to a building that is—

(a) subject to a sharing agreement, or

(b) used as mentioned in section 6. (4) of the 1969 Act.

(2) The cancellation application must be made in accordance with section 43. C.

(3) But section 43. C has effect subject to the following provisions of this section.

(4) The cancellation application may be made either—

(a) by a proprietor or trustee of the building, or

(b) by the relevant governing authority of any of the sharing churches.

(5) For that purpose, in relation to a sharing church, "relevant governing authority" means the person or persons recognised by the members of the sharing church as competent for the purpose of making an application under section 43. C in the circumstances to which this section applies.

(6) In a case where the cancellation application is made by a relevant governing authority in accordance with subsection (4)(b)—

(a) the application must be accompanied by a certificate, given by persons making the application, that they are the relevant governing authority of one of the sharing churches; and

(b) the superintendent registrar must (in addition to forwarding the application in accordance with section 43. C(3)) send a copy of that certificate to the Registrar General.

(7) The Secretary of State may by statutory instrument make regulations containing such provision supplementing this section as the Secretary of State thinks appropriate.

44. COther shared places of worship: registration and cancellation

(1) The Secretary of State may by statutory instrument make regulations about—

(a) registration applications relating to other shared places of worship;

(b) cancellation applications relating to other shared places of worship;

(c) the sharing churches' use of other shared places of worship (in cases where those places are registered under section 43. A) for the solemnization of marriages of same sex couples.

(2) The provision that may be made under subsection (1)(a) or (b) includes provision about the procedures to be followed on registration applications or cancellation applications.

(3) In this section "other shared place of worship" means a shared building—

(a) which has been certified as required by law as a place of religious worship, but

(b) to which sections 44. A and 44. B do not apply because the building is neither—

(i) subject to a sharing agreement, nor

(ii) used as mentioned in section 6. (4) of the 1969 Act.

44. DSections 44. A to 44. C: supplementary provision

(1) In sections 44. A to 44. C (and this section)—

"1969 Act" means the Sharing of Church Buildings Act 1969;

"cancellation application" means an application under section 43. C for the cancellation of the registration of a building;

"registration application" means an application under section 43. A for the registration of a building;

"sharing agreement" has the meaning given in section 1 of the 1969 Act;

"shared building" means a building that is—

- subject to a sharing agreement,

- used as mentioned in section 6. (4) of the 1969 Act, or

- otherwise shared;

"shared building provisions" means sections 44. A to 44. C;

"sharing churches" means—

- in the case of a building subject to a sharing agreement, the churches that have made the agreement;

- in the case of a building used as mentioned in section 6. (4) of the 1969 Act, the churches that so use it;

- in the case of any other shared building, the religious organisations (whether Christian or of another faith) that share it.

(2) Regulations under any of the shared building provisions may provide for a registration application relating to a shared building to be made otherwise than by the proprietor or trustee of

the building (whether or not the proprietor or trustee retains power to make such an application).

(3) Regulations under any of the shared building provisions may make provision about any of these cases—

(a) the case where a building registered under section 43. A becomes a shared building;

(b) the case where a building registered under section 43. A ceases to be a shared building;

(c) the case where a building is registered under section 43. A and there is a change in the churches which are sharing churches;

and the provision that may be made about such a case includes provision for the modification, suspension or cancellation of the registration under section 43. A.

(4) Regulations under any of the shared building provisions may make provision about the use of shared buildings for the solemnization of—

(a) marriages of same sex couples according to the usages of the Society of Friends (commonly called Quakers), and

(b) marriages of same sex couples professing the Jewish religion according to the usages of the Jews.

(5) The provision that may be made about the use of shared buildings for the solemnization of such marriages includes—

(a) provision about the giving of consent by the relevant governing authority for the purposes of a registration application or cancellation application (including provision for identifying the relevant governing authority);

(b) provision corresponding to, or applying, any provision of section 43. B (with or without modifications).

(6) Regulations under any of the shared buildings provisions may amend any England and Wales legislation.

(7) Subsections (2) to (6) do not limit the power under any of the shared building provisions to make regulations.

(8) A statutory instrument containing regulations under any of the shared building provisions may not be made unless a draft of the instrument has been laid before, and approved by resolution of, each House of Parliament.".

Commencement Information

I5. Sch. 1 para. 3 in force at 31.10.2013 for specified purposes by S.I. 2013/2789, art. 2. (a)

I6. Sch. 1 para. 3 in force at 13.3.2014 in so far as not already in force by S.I. 2014/93, art. 3. (g)

Schedule 2. Extra-territorial matters

Section 10

PART 1 English and Welsh marriages of same sex couples: treatment in Scotland and Northern Ireland

Scotland

1. (1)The Secretary of State may, by order, provide that, under the law of Scotland, a marriage of a same sex couple under the law of England and Wales is to be treated as a civil partnership formed under the law of England and Wales (and that, accordingly, the spouses are to be treated as civil partners).

(2) The Secretary of State may by order—

(a) provide for the treatment of a marriage as a civil partnership (by virtue of an order under sub-paragraph (1)) to have effect subject to provision made by the order;

(b) specify cases in which a marriage is not to be treated as a civil partnership by virtue of an order under sub-paragraph (1).

(3) The power conferred by sub-paragraph (1) may only be exercised if marriage of same sex couples is not lawful under the law of Scotland.

(4) If marriage of same sex couples becomes lawful under the law of Scotland, that does not—

(a) affect the validity of any order made under this paragraph; or

(b) prevent the revocation of any such order (with or without transitional, transitory or saving provision being made) using the powers conferred by this paragraph.

Commencement Information

I1. Sch. 2 para. 1 in force at 31.10.2013 by S.I. 2013/2789, art. 3. (d)

Northern Ireland

2. (1)Under the law of Northern Ireland, a marriage of a same sex couple under the law of England and Wales is to be treated as a civil partnership formed under the law of England and Wales (and accordingly, the spouses are to be treated as civil partners).

(2) The Secretary of State may by order—

(a) provide for the treatment of a marriage as a civil partnership (by virtue of sub-paragraph (1)) to have effect subject to provision made by the order;

(b) specify cases in which a marriage is not to be treated as a civil partnership by virtue of sub-paragraph (1).

Commencement Information

I2. Sch. 2 para. 2. (1) in force at 13.3.2014 by S.I. 2014/93, art. 3. (h)

I3. Sch. 2 para. 2. (2) in force at 31.10.2013 by S.I. 2013/2789, art. 3. (d)

Contrary provision

3. (1)The treatment of a marriage as a civil partnership by virtue of an order under paragraph 1. (1), or by virtue of paragraph 2, is subject to—

(a) any order made under paragraph 1. (2) or 2. (2), and

(b) any other contrary provision made by—

(i) the other provisions of this Act,

(ii) any other subordinate legislation made under this Act, and

(iii) any new UK legislation,

including any such contrary provision contained in amendments of existing UK legislation.

(2) In this paragraph—

"existing UK legislation" means—

 - in the case of UK legislation that is primary legislation, legislation passed before the end of the Session in which this Act is passed (excluding this Act), or

 - in the case of UK legislation that is subordinate legislation, legislation made on or before the day on which this Act is passed (excluding legislation made under this Act);

"new UK legislation" means—

 - in the case of UK legislation that is primary legislation, legislation passed after the end of the Session in which this Act is passed, or

 - in the case of UK legislation that is subordinate legislation, legislation made after the day on which this Act is passed.

Commencement Information

I4. Sch. 2 para. 3 in force at 13.3.2014 by S.I. 2014/93, art. 3. (h)

PART 2 Marriage treated as civil partnership: dissolution, annulment or separation

Order made in relation to civil partnership: validity in relation to marriage

4. (1)This paragraph applies in a case where a marriage of a same sex couple under the law of England and Wales is—

(a) by virtue of an order under paragraph 1, treated under the law of Scotland as a civil partnership, or

(b) by virtue of paragraph 2, treated under the law of Northern Ireland as a civil partnership.

(2) If—

(a) a final order is made in relation to the deemed civil partnership, and

(b) the validity of that order is recognised throughout the United Kingdom,

that order has, throughout the United Kingdom, the same effect in relation to the actual marriage that it has in relation to the deemed civil partnership.

(3) If—

(a) a separation order is made in relation to the relevant couple as parties to the deemed civil partnership, and

(b) the validity of that order is recognised throughout the United Kingdom,

that order has, throughout the United Kingdom, the same effect in relation to the couple as parties to the actual marriage that it has in relation to them as parties to the deemed civil partnership (and has effect in relation to any other persons accordingly).

(4) In this paragraph—

"actual marriage" means the marriage of the same sex couple under the law of England and Wales;

"deemed civil partnership" means the civil partnership which the actual marriage is treated as being;

"final order" means—

 - the dissolution or annulment of a civil partnership obtained from a court of civil jurisdiction in any part of the United Kingdom;

 - an overseas dissolution or annulment;

"relevant couple" means the same sex couple who are parties to the actual marriage;

"separation order" means—

 - a legal separation of the parties to a civil partnership obtained from a court of civil jurisdiction in any part of the United Kingdom;

 - an overseas legal separation of the parties to a civil partnership.

Commencement Information

I5. Sch. 2 para. 4 in force at 13.3.2014 by S.I. 2014/93, art. 3. (h)

Prospective

PART 3 England and Wales: "overseas relationships" in Civil Partnership Act 2004

Marriage not an "overseas relationship" in England and Wales

5. (1)The Civil Partnership Act 2004 is amended as follows.

(2) Section 213 (specified relationships): after subsection (1) insert—

"(1. A)But, for the purposes of the application of this Act to England and Wales, marriage is not an overseas relationship.".

Schedule 3. Interpretation of legislation

Section 11

PART 1 Existing England and Wales legislation

Interpretation of existing England and Wales legislation

1. (1)In existing England and Wales legislation—
(a) a reference to marriage is to be read as including a reference to marriage of a same sex couple;
(b) a reference to a married couple is to be read as including a reference to a married same sex couple; and
(c) a reference to a person who is married is to be read as including a reference to a person who is married to a person of the same sex.
(2) Where sub-paragraph (1) requires a reference to be read in a particular way, any related reference (such as a reference to a marriage that has ended, or a reference to a person whose marriage has ended) is to be read accordingly.
(3) For the purposes of sub-paragraphs (1) and (2) it does not matter how a reference is expressed.
Modifications etc. (not altering text)
C1. Sch. 3 paras. 1, 2 excluded by SI 2006/3432, rules 4. (4), 5. (4) (as inserted (13.3.2014) by The Marriage (Same Sex Couples) Act 2013 (Consequential and Contrary Provisions and Scotland) Order 2014 (S.I. 2014/560), art. 1. (2), Sch. 3 para. 17)
C2. Sch. 3 paras. 1-3 modified (13.3.2014) by The Marriage (Same Sex Couples) Act 2013 (Consequential and Contrary Provisions and Scotland) Order 2014 (S.I. 2014/560), art. 1. (2), Sch. 2 para. 4
C3. Sch. 3 paras. 1-3 excluded (13.3.2014) by The Marriage (Same Sex Couples) Act 2013 (Consequential and Contrary Provisions and Scotland) Order 2014 (S.I. 2014/560), art. 1. (2), Sch. 2 para. 5
C4. Sch. 3 para. 1 excluded by SI 1992/129, Sch. 2 Scheme, Sch. 1 Pt. 3 rules 1. (4), 2. (4) (as inserted (13.3.2014) by The Marriage (Same Sex Couples) Act 2013 (Consequential and Contrary Provisions and Scotland) Order 2014 (S.I. 2014/560), art. 1. (2), Sch. 3 para. 17)
C5. Sch. 3 para. 1 excluded by SI 2012/687, rules 2. A(4), 2. B(4) (as inserted (13.3.2014) by The Marriage (Same Sex Couples) Act 2013 (Consequential and Contrary Provisions and Scotland) Order 2014 (S.I. 2014/560), art. 1. (2), Sch. 3 para. 17)
C6. Sch. 3 para. 1 exluded by SI 1997/1612, regs. 42. B(4), 42. C(4) (as inserted (13.3.2014) by The Marriage (Same Sex Couples) Act 2013 (Consequential and Contrary Provisions and Scotland) Order 2014 (S.I. 2014/560), art. 1. (2), Sch. 3 para. 17)
C7. Sch. 3 paras. 1-3 excluded by SI 1987/257, reg. J1. (7) (as inserted (13.3.2014) by The Police Pensions (Amendment) Regulations 2014 (S.I. 2014/79), regs. 1. (1), 5. (c))
C8. Sch. 3 para. 1 excluded by SI 2010/990, regs. 2. A(4), 2. B(4) (as inserted (13.3.2014) by The Marriage (Same Sex Couples) Act 2013 (Consequential and Contrary Provisions and Scotland) Order 2014 (S.I. 2014/560), art. 1. (2), Sch. 3 para. 17)
Commencement Information
I1. Sch. 3 para. 1 in force at 13.3.2014 by S.I. 2014/93, art. 3. (i)

Interpretation of legislation about couples living together as if married

2. (1)In existing England and Wales legislation—

(a) a reference to persons who are not married but are living together as a married couple is to be read as including a reference to a same sex couple who are not married but are living together as a married couple;

(b) a reference to a person who is living with another person as if they were married is to be read as including a reference to a person who is living with another person of the same sex as if they were married.

(2) Where sub-paragraph (1) requires a reference to be read in a particular way, any related reference (such as a reference to persons formerly living together as a married couple) is to be read accordingly.

(3) For the purposes of sub-paragraphs (1) and (2) it does not matter how a reference is expressed.

Modifications etc. (not altering text)

C9. Sch. 3 para. 2 exluded by SI 1997/1612, regs. 42. B(4), 42. C(4) (as inserted (13.3.2014) by The Marriage (Same Sex Couples) Act 2013 (Consequential and Contrary Provisions and Scotland) Order 2014 (S.I. 2014/560), art. 1. (2), Sch. 3 para. 17)

C10. Sch. 3 para. 2 excluded by SI 2012/687, rules 2. A(4), 2. B(4) (as inserted (13.3.2014) by The Marriage (Same Sex Couples) Act 2013 (Consequential and Contrary Provisions and Scotland) Order 2014 (S.I. 2014/560), art. 1. (2), Sch. 3 para. 17)

C11. Sch. 3 para. 2 excluded by SI 2010/990, regs. 2. A(4), 2. B(4) (as inserted (13.3.2014) by The Marriage (Same Sex Couples) Act 2013 (Consequential and Contrary Provisions and Scotland) Order 2014 (S.I. 2014/560), art. 1. (2), Sch. 3 para. 17)

C12. Sch. 3 para. 2 excluded by SI 1992/129, Sch. 2 Scheme, Sch. 1 Pt. 3 rules 1. (4), 2. (4) (as inserted (13.3.2014) by The Marriage (Same Sex Couples) Act 2013 (Consequential and Contrary Provisions and Scotland) Order 2014 (S.I. 2014/560), art. 1. (2), Sch. 3 para. 17)

Commencement Information

I2. Sch. 3 para. 2 in force at 13.3.2014 by S.I. 2014/93, art. 3. (i)

3. (1)This paragraph applies to existing England and Wales legislation which deals differently with—

(a) a man and a woman living together as if married, and

(b) two men, or two women, living together as if civil partners.

(2) If two men, or two women, are living together as if married, that legislation applies to them in the way that it would apply to them if they were living together as civil partners.

Modifications etc. (not altering text)

C2. Sch. 3 paras. 1-3 modified (13.3.2014) by The Marriage (Same Sex Couples) Act 2013 (Consequential and Contrary Provisions and Scotland) Order 2014 (S.I. 2014/560), art. 1. (2), Sch. 2 para. 4

C3. Sch. 3 paras. 1-3 excluded (13.3.2014) by The Marriage (Same Sex Couples) Act 2013 (Consequential and Contrary Provisions and Scotland) Order 2014 (S.I. 2014/560), art. 1. (2), Sch. 2 para. 5

C7. Sch. 3 paras. 1-3 excluded by SI 1987/257, reg. J1. (7) (as inserted (13.3.2014) by The Police Pensions (Amendment) Regulations 2014 (S.I. 2014/79), regs. 1. (1), 5. (c))

C13. Sch. 3 para. 3 modified by SI 2006/3432, rules 4. (5), 5. (5) (as inserted (13.3.2014) by The Marriage (Same Sex Couples) Act 2013 (Consequential and Contrary Provisions and Scotland) Order 2014 (S.I. 2014/560), art. 1. (2), Sch. 3 para. 17)

C14. Sch. 3 para. 3 modified by SI 1992/1612, regs. 42. B(5), 42. C(5) (as inserted (13.3.2014) by The Marriage (Same Sex Couples) Act 2013 (Consequential and Contrary Provisions and Scotland) Order 2014 (S.I. 2014/560), art. 1. (2), Sch. 3 para. 17)

C15. Sch. 3 para. 3 modified by SI 2010/990, regs. 2. A(5), 2. B(5) (as inserted (13.3.2014) by The Marriage (Same Sex Couples) Act 2013 (Consequential and Contrary Provisions and Scotland) Order 2014 (S.I. 2014/560), art. 1. (2), Sch. 3 para. 17)

C16. Sch. 3 para. 3 modified by SI 2012/687, rules 2. A(5), 2. B(5) (as inserted (13.3.2014) by The Marriage (Same Sex Couples) Act 2013 (Consequential and Contrary Provisions and Scotland) Order 2014 (S.I. 2014/560), art. 1. (2), Sch. 3 para. 17)

C17. Sch. 3 para. 3 modified by SI 1992/129, Sch. 2 Scheme, Sch. 1 Pt. 3 rules 1. (5), 2. (5) (as

inserted (13.3.2014) by The Marriage (Same Sex Couples) Act 2013 (Consequential and Contrary Provisions and Scotland) Order 2014 (S.I. 2014/560), art. 1. (2), Sch. 3 para. 17)
Commencement Information
I3. Sch. 3 para. 3 in force at 13.3.2014 by S.I. 2014/93, art. 3. (i)

General

4. This Part of this Schedule does not limit section 11. (1) or (2).
Commencement Information
I4. Sch. 3 para. 4 in force at 13.3.2014 by S.I. 2014/93, art. 3. (i)

PART 2 New England and Wales legislation

5. (1)This paragraph applies to provision made by—
(a) this Act and any subordinate legislation made under it, or
(b) new England and Wales legislation,
including any such provision which amends existing England and Wales legislation.
(2) The following expressions have the meanings given—
(a) "husband" includes a man who is married to another man;
(b) "wife" includes a woman who is married to another woman;
(c) "widower" includes a man whose marriage to another man ended with the other man's death;
(d) "widow" includes a woman whose marriage to another woman ended with the other woman's death;
and related expressions are to be construed accordingly.
(3) A reference to marriage of same sex couples is a reference to—
(a) marriage between two men, and
(b) marriage between two women.
(4) A reference to a marriage of a same sex couple is a reference to—
(a) a marriage between two men, or
(b) a marriage between two women.
(5) A reference to a same sex couple who are not married but are living together as a married couple is a reference to—
(a) two men who are not married but are living together as a married couple, or
(b) two women who are not married but are living together as a married couple.
(6) This Part of this Schedule does not limit section 11. (1) or (2).
Commencement Information
I5. Sch. 3 para. 5 in force at 13.3.2014 by S.I. 2014/93, art. 3. (i)

Schedule 4. Effect of extension of marriage: further provision

Section 11

PART 1 Private legal instruments

Existing instruments

1. (1)Section 11 does not alter the effect of any private legal instrument made before that section comes into force.

(2) In this paragraph "private legal instrument" includes—

(a) a will,

(b) an instrument (including a private Act) which settles property,

(c) an instrument (including a private Act) which provides for the use, disposal or devolution of property, and

(d) an instrument (including a private Act) which—

(i) establishes a body, or

(ii) regulates the purposes and administration of a body,

(whether the body is incorporated or not and whether it is charitable or not);

but (with the exception of the kinds of private Act mentioned above) it does not include England and Wales legislation.

Commencement Information

I1. Sch. 4 para. 1 in force at 13.3.2014 by S.I. 2014/93, art. 3. (j)(i)

PART 2 Presumption on birth of child to married woman

Common law presumption

2. (1)Section 11 does not extend the common law presumption that a child born to a woman during her marriage is also the child of her husband.

(2) Accordingly, where a child is born to a woman during her marriage to another woman, that presumption is of no relevance to the question of who the child's parents are.

Commencement Information

I2. Sch. 4 para. 2 in force at 13.3.2014 by S.I. 2014/93, art. 3. (j)(i)

PART 3 Divorce and annulment of marriage

Divorce

3. (1)Section 1 of the Matrimonial Causes Act 1973 (divorce on breakdown of marriage) is amended as follows.

(2) After subsection (5) insert—

"(6)Only conduct between the respondent and a person of the opposite sex may constitute adultery for the purposes of this section.".

Commencement Information

I3. Sch. 4 para. 3 in force at 13.3.2014 by S.I. 2014/93, art. 3. (j)(i)

Annulment of marriage

4. (1)Section 12 of the Matrimonial Causes Act 1973 (grounds on which a marriage is voidable) is amended as follows.

(2) The existing provision of section 12 becomes subsection (1) of that section.

(3) After that subsection (1) insert—

"(2)Paragraphs (a) and (b) of subsection (1) do not apply to the marriage of a same sex couple.".

Commencement Information

I4. Sch. 4 para. 4 in force at 13.3.2014 by S.I. 2014/93, art. 3. (j)(i)

PART 4 Matrimonial proceedings

Amendment of the Domicile and Matrimonial Proceedings Act 1973.

5. The Domicile and Matrimonial Proceedings Act 1973 is amended as follows.
Commencement Information
I5. Sch. 4 para. 5 in force at 31.10.2013 for specified purposes by S.I. 2013/2789, art. 2. (b)
I6. Sch. 4 para. 5 in force at 13.3.2014 in so far as not already in force by S.I. 2014/93, art. 3. (j)(i)
6. (1)Section 5 (jurisdiction of High Court and county courts) is amended in accordance with this paragraph.
(2) Subsection (1): after "entertain" insert " any of the following proceedings in relation to a marriage of a man and a woman ".
(3) After subsection (5) insert—
"(5. A)Schedule A1 (jurisdiction in relation to marriage of same sex couples) has effect.".
(4) Subsection (6): after "Wales" insert " (whether the proceedings are in respect of the marriage of a man and a woman or the marriage of a same sex couple) ".
Commencement Information
I7. Sch. 4 para. 6 in force at 13.3.2014 by S.I. 2014/93, art. 3. (j)(i)
7. Section 6 (miscellaneous amendments, transitional provision and savings), subsection (3): after "Act" (in the first place) insert " , or by virtue of Schedule A1 to this Act, ".
Commencement Information
I8. Sch. 4 para. 7 in force at 13.3.2014 by S.I. 2014/93, art. 3. (j)(i)
8. Before Schedule 1 insert— "SCHEDULE A1 Jurisdiction in relation to marriage of same sex couples
1. Introduction
This Schedule shall have effect, subject to section 6. (3) and (4), with respect to the jurisdiction of the court to entertain any of the following proceedings in relation to a marriage of a same sex couple—
(a) proceedings for divorce, judicial separation or nullity of marriage;
(b) proceedings for an order which ends a marriage on the ground that one of the couple is dead; and
(c) proceedings for a declaration of validity.
2. Divorce, judicial separation or annulment
(1) The court has jurisdiction to entertain proceedings for divorce or judicial separation if (and only if)—
(a) the court has jurisdiction under regulations under paragraph 5,
(b) no court has, or is recognised as having, jurisdiction under regulations under paragraph 5 and either of the married same sex couple is domiciled in England and Wales on the date when the proceedings are begun, or
(c) the following conditions are met—
(i) the two people concerned married each other under the law of England and Wales,
(ii) no court has, or is recognised as having, jurisdiction under regulations under paragraph 5, and
(iii) it appears to the court to be in the interests of justice to assume jurisdiction in the case.
(2) The court has jurisdiction to entertain proceedings for nullity of marriage if (and only if)—
(a) the court has jurisdiction under regulations under paragraph 5,
(b) no court has, or is recognised as having, jurisdiction under regulations under paragraph 5 and either of the married same sex couple—
(i) is domiciled in England and Wales on the date when the proceedings are begun, or
(ii) died before that date and either was at death domiciled in England and Wales or had been

habitually resident in England and Wales throughout the period of 1 year ending with the date of death, or

(c) the following conditions are met—

(i) the two people concerned married each other under the law of England and Wales,

(ii) no court has, or is recognised as having, jurisdiction under regulations under paragraph 5, and

(iii) it appears to the court to be in the interests of justice to assume jurisdiction in the case.

(3) At any time when proceedings are pending in respect of which the court has jurisdiction by virtue of sub-paragraph (1) or (2) (or this sub-paragraph), the court also has jurisdiction to entertain other proceedings, in respect of the same marriage, for divorce, judicial separation or nullity of marriage, even though that jurisdiction would not be exercisable under subsection (1) or (2).

3. Presumption of death order

The court has jurisdiction to entertain proceedings for an order which ends a marriage on the ground that one of the couple is dead on an application made by the other of the couple ("the applicant") if (and only if)—

(a) at the time the application is made, the High Court does not have jurisdiction to entertain an application by the applicant under section 1 of the Presumption of Death Act 2013 for a declaration that the applicant's spouse is presumed to be dead, and

(b) the two people concerned married each other under the law of England and Wales and it appears to the court to be in the interests of justice to assume jurisdiction in the case.

4. Declaration of validity

The court has jurisdiction to entertain an application for a declaration of validity if (and only if)—

(a) either of the parties to the marriage to which the application relates—

(i) is domiciled in England and Wales on the date of the application,

(ii) has been habitually resident in England and Wales throughout the period of 1 year ending with that date, or

(iii) died before that date and either was at death domiciled in England and Wales or had been habitually resident in England and Wales throughout the period of 1 year ending with the date of death, or

(b) the two people concerned married each other under the law of England and Wales and it appears to the court to be in the interests of justice to assume jurisdiction in the case.

5. Power to make provision corresponding to EC Regulation 2201/2003

(1) The Lord Chancellor may by regulations make provision—

(a) as to the jurisdiction of courts in England and Wales in proceedings for the divorce of, or annulment of the marriage of, a same sex couple or for judicial separation of a married same sex couple where one of the couple—

(i) is or has been habitually resident in a member State,

(ii) is a national of a member State, or

(iii) is domiciled in a part of the United Kingdom or the Republic of Ireland, and

(b) as to the recognition in England and Wales of any judgment of a court of another member State which orders the divorce of, or annulment of a marriage of, a same sex couple or the judicial separation of a married same sex couple.

(2) The regulations may in particular make provision corresponding to that made by Council Regulation (EC) No 2201/2003 of 27th November 2003 in relation to jurisdiction and the recognition and enforcement of judgments in matrimonial matters.

(3) The regulations may provide that for the purposes of the regulations "member State" means—

(a) all member States with the exception of such member States as are specified in the regulations, or

(b) such member States as are specified in the regulations.

(4) The regulations may make provision under sub-paragraph (1)(b) which applies even if the date of the divorce, annulment or judicial separation is earlier than the date on which this paragraph comes into force.

(5) Regulations under this paragraph are to be made by statutory instrument.

(6) A statutory instrument containing regulations under this paragraph may not be made unless a draft of the statutory instrument containing the order or regulations has been laid before, and approved by resolution of, each House of Parliament.

6. Interpretation

In this Schedule "declaration of validity" means—

    (a) a declaration as to the validity of a marriage,

    (b) a declaration as to the subsistence of a marriage, or

    (c) a declaration as to the validity of a divorce, annulment or judicial separation obtained outside England and Wales in respect of a marriage.".

Commencement Information

I9. Sch. 4 para. 8 in force at 31.10.2013 for specified purposes by S.I. 2013/2789, art. 2. (b)

I10. Sch. 4 para. 8 in force at 13.3.2014 in so far as not already in force by S.I. 2014/93, art. 3. (j)(i)

9. Schedule 1 (staying of matrimonial proceedings in England and Wales: interpretation), paragraph 2: after "kinds" insert " (whether relating to a marriage of a man and a woman or a marriage of a same sex couple) ".

Commencement Information

I11. Sch. 4 para. 9 in force at 13.3.2014 by S.I. 2014/93, art. 3. (j)(i)

Transitory provision until commencement of Presumption of Death Act 2013.

10. (1)This paragraph applies if section 1 of the Presumption of Death Act 2013 has not come into force at the time when the amendments of the Domicile and Matrimonial Proceedings Act 1973 made by the other provisions of this Part of this Schedule come into force.

(2) Schedule A1 to the Domicile and Matrimonial Proceedings Act 1973 has effect with the following modifications until section 1 of the Presumption of Death Act 2013 comes into force.

(3) Paragraph 1 has effect with the following provision substituted for paragraph (b)—

    "(b)proceedings for death to be presumed and a marriage to be dissolved in pursuance of section 19 of the Matrimonial Causes Act 1973; and".

(4) Schedule A1 has effect with the following provision substituted for paragraph 3—

"3. The court has jurisdiction to entertain proceedings for death to be presumed and a marriage to be dissolved if (and only if)—

(a) the applicant is domiciled in England and Wales on the date when the proceedings are begun,

(b) the applicant was habitually resident in England and Wales throughout the period of 1 year ending with that date, or

(c) the two people concerned married each other under the law of England and Wales and it appears to the court to be in the interests of justice to assume jurisdiction in the case.".

Commencement Information

I12. Sch. 4 para. 10 in force at 13.3.2014 by S.I. 2014/93, art. 3. (j)(i)

PART 5 State pensions

Category B retirement pension for married person

F1 11. . . . .

Amendments (Textual)

F1. Sch. 4 para. 11 omitted (6.4.2016 unless brought into force earlier by an order under s. 56. (1) of the amending Act) by virtue of Pensions Act 2014 (c. 19), s. 56. (4), Sch. 12 para. 77 (with Sch. 12 para. 87. (1)(2))

Category B retirement pension for widows and widowers

F2 12. . . . .
Amendments (Textual)
F2. Sch. 4 para. 12 omitted (6.4.2016 unless brought into force earlier by an order under s. 56. (1) of the amending Act) by virtue of Pensions Act 2014 (c. 19), s. 56. (4), Sch. 12 para. 77 (with Sch. 12 para. 87. (1)(2))

Category B retirement pension for widowers

F3 13. . . . .
Amendments (Textual)
F3. Sch. 4 para. 13 omitted (6.4.2016 unless brought into force earlier by an order under s. 56. (1) of the amending Act) by virtue of Pensions Act 2014 (c. 19), s. 56. (4), Sch. 12 para. 77 (with Sch. 12 para. 87. (1)(2))

Graduated retirement benefit

14. (1)Section 62 of the Social Security Contributions and Benefits Act 1992 (graduated retirement benefit) is amended as follows.
(2) Subsection (1): after paragraph (ac) insert—
   "(ad)for extending section 37 of that Act (increase of woman's retirement pension by reference to her late husband's graduated retirement benefit) to—
(i) men and their late husbands, and
(ii) women and their late wives,
and for that section (except subsection (5)) so to apply as it applies to women and their late husbands;
   (ae) for extending section 37 of that Act (increase of woman's retirement pension by reference to her late husband's graduated retirement benefit) to—
(i) men and their late husbands, and
(ii) women and their late wives,
who attained pensionable age before 6th April 2010 and for that section (except subsection (5)) so to apply as it applies to men and their late wives;".
(3) After subsection (2) insert—
"(3)In relevant gender change cases, women and their late wives are to be treated for the purposes of sections 36 and 37 of the National Insurance Act 1965 in the same way as women and their late husbands.
(4) For that purpose "relevant gender change case", in relation to a woman ("the pensioner") and her late wife, means a case where—
   (a) the late wife was, at the time of her death, a woman by virtue of a full gender recognition certificate having been issued under the Gender Recognition Act 2004, and
   (b) the marriage of the pensioner and her late wife subsisted before the time when the certificate was issued."
Commencement Information
I13. Sch. 4 para. 14 in force at 31.10.2013 for specified purposes by S.I. 2013/2789, art. 2. (b)
I14. Sch. 4 para. 14 in force at 13.3.2014 for specified purposes by S.I. 2014/93, art. 3. (j)(ii)
I15. Sch. 4 para. 14 in force at 10.12.2014 in so far as not already in force by S.I. 2014/3169, art. 2

Adult dependency increases

15. (1)In a case where a full gender recognition certificate is issued to a person under the Gender Recognition Act 2004—

(a) section 83 of the 1992 Act (pension increase (wife)) does not cease to apply by virtue of the change of gender; and

(b) in the continued application of section 83 in such a case, references to a pension payable to a man, or references to his wife, are to be construed accordingly.

(2) In a case where a full gender recognition certificate is issued to a person under the Gender Recognition Act 2004—

(a) section 84 of the 1992 Act (pension increase (husband)) does not cease to apply by virtue of the change of gender; and

(b) in the continued application of section 84 in such a case, references to a pension payable to a woman, or references to her husband, are to be construed accordingly.

(3) In this paragraph "the 1992 Act" means the Social Security Contributions and Benefits Act 1992.

Commencement Information

I16. Sch. 4 para. 15 in force at 10.12.2014 by S.I. 2014/3169, art. 2

Converted civil partnerships

F416. . . . .

Amendments (Textual)

F4. Sch. 4 para. 16 omitted (6.4.2016 unless brought into force earlier by an order under s. 56. (1) of the amending Act) by virtue of Pensions Act 2014 (c. 19), s. 56. (4), Sch. 12 para. 77 (with Sch. 12 para. 87. (1)(2))

PART 6 Occupational pensions and survivor benefits

Benefits dependent on marriage of same sex couples

17. (1)Paragraph 18 of Schedule 9 to the Equality Act 2010 (work: exceptions) is amended as follows.

(2) Sub-paragraph (1): for "married" substitute " within sub-paragraph (1. A) ".

(3) After sub-paragraph (1) insert—

"(1. A)A person is within this sub-paragraph if the person is—

   (a) a man who is married to a woman, or

   (b) a woman who is married to a man, or

   (c) married to a person of the same sex in a relevant gender change case.

(1. B)The reference in sub-paragraph (1. A)(c) to a relevant gender change case is a reference to a case where—

   (a) the married couple were of the opposite sex at the time of their marriage, and

   (b) a full gender recognition certificate has been issued to one of the couple under the Gender Recognition Act 2004.".

Commencement Information

I17. Sch. 4 para. 17 in force at 13.3.2014 for specified purposes by S.I. 2014/93, art. 3. (j)(iii)

Pension Schemes Act 1993.

18. The Pension Schemes Act 1993 is amended in accordance with paragraphs 19 to 26.

Commencement Information

I18. Sch. 4 para. 18 in force at 13.3.2014 for specified purposes by S.I. 2014/93, art. 3. (j)(iv)

119. Sch. 4 para. 18 in force at 30.6.2014 for specified purposes by S.I. 2014/1662, art. 3. (b)

120. Sch. 4 para. 18 in force at 10.12.2014 in so far as not already in force by S.I. 2014/3169, art. 2

19. In section 8. (2) (meaning of certain terms), in the definition of "guaranteed minimum pension", after "widower's" insert ", surviving same sex spouse's".

Commencement Information

121. Sch. 4 para. 19 in force at 13.3.2014 by S.I. 2014/93, art. 3. (j)(v)

20. (1)Section 17 (minimum pensions for widows and widowers) is amended as follows.

(2) Subsection (2)—

(a) paragraph (a): after "man" insert " , or a woman in a relevant gender change case, ";

(b) after paragraph (c) insert—

"(d)if the earner is a man who has a guaranteed minimum under that section, the weekly rate of the widower's pension will not be less than the surviving same sex spouse's guaranteed minimum;

(e) if the earner is a woman (other than in a relevant gender change case) who has a guaranteed minimum under that section, the weekly rate of the widow's pension will not be less than the surviving same sex spouse's guaranteed minimum.".

(3) Subsection (4): after "partner's" insert "or surviving same sex spouse's".

(4) Subsection (5): at the beginning insert " In the case of a woman who is the widow of a man, ".

(5) Subsection (6)—

(a) at the beginning insert " In any other case, ";

(b) after "widower's" insert ", widow's".

(6) After subsection (9) insert—

"(10)In relation to an earner who is a woman, a reference in this section to a relevant gender change case is a reference to a case where—

(a) the earner is a woman by virtue of a full gender recognition certificate having been issued under the Gender Recognition Act 2004, and

(b) the marriage of the earner and her widow (that ends with the earner's death) subsisted before the time when the certificate was issued.

(11) This section is subject to regulations under section 38. A.".

Commencement Information

122. Sch. 4 para. 20 in force at 13.3.2014 for specified purposes by S.I. 2014/93, art. 3. (j)(vi)

123. Sch. 4 para. 20 in force at 10.12.2014 in so far as not already in force by S.I. 2014/3169, art. 2

21. (1)Section 24. D (survivors' benefits) is amended as follows.

(2) Subsection (2): after "earner" insert " is a man married to a woman or a woman married to a woman in a relevant gender change case, and the earner ".

(3) Subsection (3)—

(a) after "earner" insert " is a married woman (other than in a relevant gender change case), a man married to a man, or a civil partner, and the earner ";

(b) after "widower" insert " , widow ".

(4) After subsection (3) insert—

"(4)In relation to an earner who is a woman, a reference in this section to a relevant gender change case is a reference to a case where—

(a) the earner is a woman by virtue of a full gender recognition certificate having been issued under the Gender Recognition Act 2004, and

(b) the marriage of the earner and her widow (that ends with the earner's death) subsisted before the time when the certificate was issued.

(5) This section is subject to regulations under section 38. A.".

Commencement Information

124. Sch. 4 para. 21 in force at 13.3.2014 for specified purposes by S.I. 2014/93, art. 3. (j)(vi)

125. Sch. 4 para. 21 in force at 10.12.2014 in so far as not already in force by S.I. 2014/3169, art. 2

22. (1)Section 37 (alteration of rules of contracted-out schemes) is amended as follows.

(2) For subsection (4) substitute—

"(4)The reference in subsection (3) to a person entitled to receive benefits under a scheme includes a person who is so entitled by virtue of a qualifying relationship only in such cases as may be prescribed.

(5) For that purpose a person is entitled to receive benefits by virtue of a qualifying relationship if the person is so entitled by virtue of being—

    (a) the widower of a female earner;

    (b) the widower of a male earner;

    (c) the widow of a female earner, except where it is a relevant gender change case; or

    (d) the survivor of a civil partnership with an earner.

(6) In relation to a widow of a female earner, the reference in subsection (5)(c) to a relevant gender change case is a reference to a case where—

    (a) the earner is a woman by virtue of a full gender recognition certificate having been issued under the Gender Recognition Act 2004, and

    (b) the marriage of the earner and her widow (that ends with the earner's death) subsisted before the time when the certificate was issued.

(7) This section is subject to regulations under section 38. A.".

Commencement Information

I26. Sch. 4 para. 22 in force at 13.3.2014 for specified purposes by S.I. 2014/93, art. 3. (j)(vi)

I27. Sch. 4 para. 22 in force at 10.12.2014 in so far as not already in force by S.I. 2014/3169, art. 2

23. Before section 39 insert—

"38. ARegulations about relevant gender change cases

(1) The Secretary of State may, by regulations, make provision for—

    (a) section 17,

    (b) section 24. D, or

    (c) section 37,

to have its special effect in relevant gender change cases only if conditions prescribed in the regulations are met.

(2) Regulations under subsection (1) may, in particular, prescribe conditions that relate to the provision of information by—

    (a) one or both of the members of married same sex couples, or

    (b) the survivors of such couples.

(3) The Secretary of State may, by regulations, make further provision about cases where (because of regulations under subsection (1))—

    (a) section 17,

    (b) section 24. D, or

    (c) section 37,

does not have its special effect in relevant gender change cases.

(4) Regulations under subsection (3) may, in particular, provide for the section in question to have its ordinary effect in relevant gender change cases.

(5) Regulations under subsection (1) or (3) may, in particular, modify or disapply any enactment that concerns information relating to—

    (a) the gender or sex of a person, or

    (b) the change of gender or sex of a person,

including any enactment that concerns requests for, or disclosure of, such information.

(6) In this section, in relation to section 17, 24. D or 37—

    (a) "relevant gender change case" has the same meaning as in that section;

    (b) "special effect" means the effect which the section has (if regulations under subsection (1) of this section are ignored) in relation to relevant gender change cases, insofar as that effect is different from the section's ordinary effect;

    (c) "ordinary effect" means the effect which the section has in relation to same sex married couples in cases that are not relevant gender change cases.".

Commencement Information

I28. Sch. 4 para. 23 in force at 30.6.2014 by S.I. 2014/1662, art. 3. (a)

24. In section 47 (further provisions about effect of entitlement to guaranteed minimum pension on payment of social security benefits), in subsection (1) after "widower" insert " , surviving same

sex spouse ".

Commencement Information

I29. Sch. 4 para. 24 in force at 13.3.2014 by S.I. 2014/93, art. 3. (j)(vii)

25. In section 84 (basis of revaluation), in subsection (5), after "widower" insert " , surviving same sex spouse ".

Commencement Information

I30. Sch. 4 para. 25 in force at 13.3.2014 by S.I. 2014/93, art. 3. (j)(vii)

26. In Schedule 3 (methods of revaluing accrued pension benefits), in paragraph 1. (1. E)(b), after "widower" insert " , surviving same sex spouse ".

Commencement Information

I31. Sch. 4 para. 26 in force at 13.3.2014 by S.I. 2014/93, art. 3. (j)(vii)

PART 7 Provisions which limit equivalence of all marriages etc

Contrary provision

27. (1)The relevant enactments are subject to—

(a) the preceding provisions of this Schedule, and

(b) any order under sub-paragraph (3).

(2) The relevant enactments are subject to any other contrary provision made by—

(a) the other provisions of this Act,

(b) any other subordinate legislation made under this Act, and

(c) any new England and Wales legislation,

including any such contrary provision contained in amendments of existing England and Wales legislation.

(3) The Secretary of State may by order—

(a) provide that a relevant enactment has effect subject to provision made by the order, or

(b) specify cases in which a relevant enactment does not apply.

(4) In this paragraph "relevant enactment" means—

(a) section 11. (1) and (2) and Schedule 3 (equivalence of all marriages in law), or

(b) section 9. (6)(b) (marriage arising from conversion of civil partnership treated as having subsisted from formation of civil partnership).

Commencement Information

I32. Sch. 4 para. 27. (1)(2) in force at 13.3.2014 by S.I. 2014/93, art. 3. (j)(viii)

I33. Sch. 4 para. 27. (3)(4) in force at 31.10.2013 by S.I. 2013/2789, art. 3. (e)

Schedule 5. Change of gender of married persons or civil partners

Section 12

PART 1 Applications by married persons and civil partners

Introduction

1. The Gender Recognition Act 2004 is amended in accordance with this Part of this Schedule.

Commencement Information

I1. Sch. 5 para. 1 in force at 30.6.2014 for specified purposes by S.I. 2014/1662, art. 2. (b)

I2. Sch. 5 para. 1 in force at 10.12.2014 in so far as not already in force by S.I. 2014/3169, art. 2

Evidence

2. Section 3 (evidence): after subsection (6) insert—

"(6. A)If the applicant is married, an application under section 1. (1) must include a statutory declaration as to whether the marriage is a marriage under the law of England and Wales, of Scotland, of Northern Ireland, or of a country or territory outside the United Kingdom.

(6. B)If the applicant is married, and the marriage is a protected marriage, an application under section 1. (1) must also include—

(a) a statutory declaration by the applicant's spouse that the spouse consents to the marriage continuing after the issue of a full gender recognition certificate ("a statutory declaration of consent") (if the spouse has made such a declaration), or

(b) a statutory declaration by the applicant that the applicant's spouse has not made a statutory declaration of consent (if that is the case).

(6. C)If an application includes a statutory declaration of consent by the applicant's spouse, the Gender Recognition Panel must give the spouse notice that the application has been made.".

Commencement Information

I3. Sch. 5 para. 2 in force at 10.12.2014 by S.I. 2014/3169, art. 2

Successful applications

3. Section 4 (successful applications): for subsections (2) and (3) substitute—

"(2)The certificate is to be a full gender recognition certificate if—

(a) the applicant is neither a civil partner nor married,

(b) the applicant is a party to a protected marriage and the applicant's spouse consents to the marriage continuing after the issue of a full gender recognition certificate, or

(c) the applicant is a party to a protected civil partnership and the Panel has decided to issue a full gender recognition certificate to the other party to the civil partnership.

(3) The certificate is to be an interim gender recognition certificate if—

(a) the applicant is a party to a protected marriage and the applicant's spouse does not consent to the marriage continuing after the issue of a full gender recognition certificate,

(b) the applicant is a party to a marriage that is not a protected marriage,

(c) the applicant is a party to a protected civil partnership and the other party to the civil partnership has not made an application under section 1. (1),

(d) the applicant is a party to a protected civil partnership and the Panel has decided not to issue a full gender recognition certificate to the other party to the civil partnership, or

(e) the applicant is a party to a civil partnership that is not a protected civil partnership.

(3. A)If a Gender Recognition Panel issues a full gender recognition certificate under this section to an applicant who is a party to a protected marriage, the Panel must give the applicant's spouse notice of the issue of the certificate.

(3. B)Subsection (2)(c) is subject to section 5. B.".

Commencement Information

I4. Sch. 5 para. 3 in force at 10.12.2014 by S.I. 2014/3169, art. 2

Issue of full certificate after interim certificate: applicant married

4. After section 4 insert—

"Issue of full certificate after interim certificate: applicant married

4. AMarried person with interim certificate: issue of full certificate

(1) A Gender Recognition Panel must issue a full gender recognition certificate to a person in either of the following cases.

(2) Case A is where, on an application by the person, the Panel is satisfied that—

    (a) an interim gender recognition certificate has been issued to the person;

    (b) the person was a party to a protected marriage at the time when the interim gender recognition certificate was issued;

    (c) the person is a party to a protected marriage; and

    (d) the person's spouse now consents to the marriage continuing after the issue of the full gender recognition certificate.

(3) Case B is where, on an application by the person, the Panel is satisfied that—

    (a) an interim gender recognition certificate has been issued to the person;

    (b) the person was a party to a civil partnership at the time when the interim gender recognition certificate was issued;

    (c) a conversion application has been made within the period of six months beginning with the day on which that certificate was issued;

    (d) the conversion application has resulted in the civil partnership being converted into a marriage;

    (e) the person is a party to that marriage; and

    (f) the person's spouse consents to the marriage continuing after the issue of the full gender recognition certificate.

(4) If, on an application under subsection (2) or (3), the Panel is not satisfied as mentioned in that subsection, the Panel must reject the application.

(5) An application under subsection (2) must be made within the period of six months beginning with the day on which the interim gender recognition certificate is issued.

(6) An application under subsection (3) must be made within the period of six months beginning with the day on which the civil partnership is converted into a marriage.

(7) An application under subsection (2) or (3) must include a statutory declaration of consent made by the person's spouse.

(8) An application under subsection (3) must also include—

    (a) evidence of the date on which the conversion application was made, and

    (b) evidence of the conversion of the civil partnership into a marriage.

(9) If an application is made under this section, the Gender Recognition Panel must give the applicant's spouse—

    (a) notice of the application; and

    (b) if the Panel grants the application, notice of the issue of the full gender recognition certificate.

(10) In this section "conversion application" means an application for the conversion of a civil partnership into a marriage under regulations under section 9 of the Marriage (Same Sex Couples) Act 2013.

4. BApplication under section 4. A: death of spouse

(1) In a case where an application is made under section 4. A(2) or (3) and the applicant's spouse dies before the application is determined—

    (a) the application is to be treated as an application, made under section 5. (2) in a case where a spouse has died, for a full gender recognition certificate to be issued; and

    (b) that application is to be treated as having been made at the time when the application under section 4. A was made.

(2) The Gender Recognition Panel determining the application must specify the period within which the applicant is to produce the required evidence in support of the new application.

(3) In this section—

"new application" means the application under section 5. (2) which the person is, by virtue of subsection (1), treated as having made;

"required evidence" means the evidence required by section 5. (4).

Issue of full certificate after interim certificate: applicant no longer married or civil partner ".
Commencement Information
I5. Sch. 5 para. 4 in force at 10.12.2014 by S.I. 2014/3169, art. 2

Applications by both civil partners

5. After section 5. A insert—
"Other provision about applications and certificates
5. BApplications by both civil partners
(1) This section applies where the Panel decides to issue a full gender recognition certificate to a party to a protected civil partnership.
(2) The Panel must not issue the full gender recognition certificate to that person unless the Panel issues a full gender recognition certificate to the other party to the protected civil partnership.
(3) In such a case, the Panel must issue both certificates on the same day.
(4) Those certificates take effect at the beginning of the day on which they are issued.".
Commencement Information
I6. Sch. 5 para. 5 in force at 10.12.2014 by S.I. 2014/3169, art. 2

Errors in certificates

6. Section 6 (errors in certificates)—
(a) for the title substitute " Errors ";
(b) for subsection (1) substitute—
"(1)Where a gender recognition certificate has been issued to a person, the person or the Secretary of State may make an application for—
    (a) an interim gender recognition certificate, on the ground that a full gender recognition certificate has incorrectly been issued instead of an interim certificate;
    (b) a full gender recognition certificate, on the ground that an interim gender recognition certificate has incorrectly been issued instead of a full certificate; or
    (c) a corrected certificate, on the ground that the certificate which has been issued contains an error.";
(c) subsection (3): for paragraph (a) substitute—
    "(a)must grant the application if satisfied that the ground on which the application is made is correct, and";
(d) subsection (4): for "a corrected" substitute " a correct, or a corrected, ".
Commencement Information
I7. Sch. 5 para. 6 in force at 10.12.2014 by S.I. 2014/3169, art. 2

Applications: supplementary

7. Section 7 (applications: supplementary), subsection (1): after "1. (1)," insert " 4. A, ".
Commencement Information
I8. Sch. 5 para. 7 in force at 10.12.2014 by S.I. 2014/3169, art. 2

Appeals etc

8. Section 8 (appeals etc)—
(a) subsection (1): after "1. (1)," insert " 4. A, ";
(b) subsection (5): after "1. (1)," insert " 4. A, ";
(c) after subsection (5) insert—
"(5. A)If an application under section 1. (1), 4. A, 5. (2), 5. A(2) or 6. (1) is granted, the applicant's

44

spouse may apply to the High Court or Court of Session to quash the decision to grant the application on the grounds that its grant was secured by fraud.";

(d) subsection (6): after "subsection (5)" insert " or an application under subsection (5. A) ".

Commencement Information

I9. Sch. 5 para. 8 in force at 10.12.2014 by S.I. 2014/3169, art. 2

Registration

9. (1)Section 10 (registration): after subsection (1) insert—

"(1. A)Where a full gender recognition certificate is issued to a person who is a party to—

   (a) a marriage under the law of England and Wales, or

   (b) a civil partnership under that law,

the Secretary of State must send a copy of the certificate to the Registrar General for England and Wales.".

(2) Schedule 3 (registration), Part 1 (England and Wales): at end insert—

"Registration of marriages and civil partnerships

11. A(1)The Registrar General may make regulations about—

(a) the registration of qualifying marriages, and

(b) the registration of qualifying civil partnerships.

(2) The regulations may, in particular, provide for the maintenance of—

(a) a separate register in relation to qualifying marriages, and

(b) a separate register in relation to qualifying civil partnerships.

(3) In this paragraph—

"qualifying civil partnership" means a civil partnership under the law of England and Wales in a case where a full gender recognition certificate has been issued to each of the civil partners;

"qualifying marriage" means a marriage under the law of England and Wales in a case where a full gender recognition certificate has been issued to one, or each, of the spouses.".

Commencement Information

I10. Sch. 5 para. 9 in force at 30.6.2014 for specified purposes by S.I. 2014/1662, art. 2. (b)

I11. Sch. 5 para. 9 in force at 10.12.2014 in so far as not already in force by S.I. 2014/3169, art. 2

Change in gender of party to marriage

10. After section 11 insert—

"11. AChange in gender of party to marriage

(1) This section applies in relation to a protected marriage if (by virtue of section 4. (2)(b) or 4. A) a full gender recognition certificate is issued to a party to the marriage.

(2) The continuity of the protected marriage is not affected by the relevant change in gender.

(3) If the protected marriage is a foreign marriage—

   (a) the continuity of the marriage continues by virtue of subsection (2) notwithstanding any impediment under the proper law of the marriage;

   (b) the proper law of the marriage is not affected by its continuation by virtue of subsection (2).

(4) In this section—

"foreign marriage" means a marriage under the law of a country or territory outside the United Kingdom;

"impediment" means anything which affects the continuation of a marriage merely by virtue of the relevant change in gender;

"proper law", in relation to a protected marriage, means the law of the country or territory under which the marriage was entered into;

"relevant change in gender" means the change or changes of gender occurring by virtue of the issue of the full gender recognition certificate or certificates.".

Commencement Information

Change in gender of civil partners

11. After section 11. A (inserted by paragraph 10) insert—
"11. BChange in gender of civil partners
The continuity of a civil partnership is not affected by the issuing of full gender recognition
certificates (by virtue of section 4. (2)(c)) to both civil partners.".
Commencement Information
I13. Sch. 5 para. 11 in force at 10.12.2014 by S.I. 2014/3169, art. 2

Foreign gender change and marriage

12. Section 21 (foreign gender change and marriage)—
(a) after subsection (1) insert—
"(1. A)Subsections (2) to (5) apply only in Scotland and Northern Ireland.";
(b) subsection (2): for "Accordingly," substitute " In accordance with subsection (1), ".
Commencement Information
I14. Sch. 5 para. 12 in force at 10.12.2014 by S.I. 2014/3169, art. 2

Prohibition on disclosure of information

13. Section 22 (prohibition on disclosure of information), subsection (2)(a): after "section" insert "
4. A, ".
Commencement Information
I15. Sch. 5 para. 13 in force at 10.12.2014 by S.I. 2014/3169, art. 2

Interpretation

14. Section 25 (interpretation)—
(a) after the definition of "Gender Recognition Panel" insert—
""protected civil partnership" means a civil partnership under the law of England and Wales;
"protected marriage" means—
   (a) a marriage under the law of England and Wales, or
   (b) a marriage under the law of a country or territory outside the United Kingdom,";
(b) after the definition of "registered psychologist" insert—
""statutory declaration of consent" has the meaning given by section 3. (6. B)(a),".
Commencement Information
I16. Sch. 5 para. 14 in force at 10.12.2014 by S.I. 2014/3169, art. 2

PART 2 Alternative grounds for granting applications for gender recognition certificates

Introduction

15. The Gender Recognition Act 2004 is amended in accordance with this Part of this Schedule.
Commencement Information
I17. Sch. 5 para. 15 in force at 10.12.2014 by S.I. 2014/3169, art. 2

Alternative grounds for granting applications

16. Section 2 (determination of applications): after subsection (3) insert—
"(3. A)This section does not apply to an application under section 1. (1)(a) which states that it is an application for a certificate to be granted in accordance with section 3. A."
Commencement Information
I18. Sch. 5 para. 16 in force at 10.12.2014 by S.I. 2014/3169, art. 2
17. After section 3 insert—
"3. AAlternative grounds for granting applications
(1) This section applies to an application under section 1. (1)(a) which states that it is an application for a certificate to be granted in accordance with this section.
(2) The Panel must grant the application if satisfied that the applicant complies with the requirements imposed by and under section 3. B and meets the conditions in subsections (3) to (6).
(3) The first condition is that the applicant was a party to a protected marriage or a protected civil partnership on or before the date the application was made.
(4) The second condition is that the applicant—
    (a) was living in the acquired gender six years before the commencement of section 12 of the Marriage (Same Sex Couples) Act 2013,
    (b) continued to live in the acquired gender until the date the application was made, and
    (c) intends to continue to live in the acquired gender until death.
(5) The third condition is that the applicant—
    (a) has or has had gender dysphoria, or
    (b) has undergone surgical treatment for the purpose of modifying sexual characteristics.
(6) The fourth condition is that the applicant is ordinarily resident in England, Wales or Scotland.
(7) The Panel must reject the application if not required by subsection (2) to grant it."
Commencement Information
I19. Sch. 5 para. 17 in force at 10.12.2014 by S.I. 2014/3169, art. 2

Evidence for granting applications on alternative grounds

18. Section 3 (evidence): after subsection (8) insert—
"(9)This section does not apply to an application under section 1. (1)(a) which states that it is an application for a certificate to be granted in accordance with section 3. A."
Commencement Information
I20. Sch. 5 para. 18 in force at 10.12.2014 by S.I. 2014/3169, art. 2
19. After section 3. A (inserted by paragraph 17) insert—
"3. BEvidence for granting applications on alternative grounds
(1) This section applies to an application under section 1. (1)(a) which states that it is an application for a certificate to be granted in accordance with section 3. A.
(2) The application must include either—
    (a) a report made by a registered medical practitioner, or
    (b) a report made by a registered psychologist practising in the field of gender dysphoria.
(3) If the application is based on the applicant having or having had gender dysphoria—
    (a) the reference in subsection (2) to a registered medical practitioner is to one practising in the field of gender dysphoria, and
    (b) that subsection is not complied with unless the report includes details of the diagnosis of the applicant's gender dysphoria.
(4) Subsection (2) is not complied with in a case where—
    (a) the applicant has undergone or is undergoing treatment for the purpose of modifying sexual characteristics, or
    (b) treatment for that purpose has been prescribed or planned for the applicant,
unless the report required by that subsection includes details of it.

47

(5) The application must also include a statutory declaration by the applicant that the applicant meets the conditions in section 3. A(3) and (4).

(6) The application must include—

(a) a statutory declaration as to whether or not the applicant is married or a civil partner,

(b) any other information or evidence required by an order made by the Secretary of State, and

(c) any other information or evidence which the Panel which is to determine the application may require,

and may include any other information or evidence which the applicant wishes to include.

(7) If the applicant is married, the application must include a statutory declaration as to whether the marriage is a marriage under the law of England and Wales, of Scotland, of Northern Ireland, or of a country or territory outside the United Kingdom.

(8) If the applicant is married, and the marriage is a protected marriage, the application must also include—

(a) a statutory declaration of consent by the applicant's spouse (if the spouse has made such a declaration), or

(b) a statutory declaration by the applicant that the applicant's spouse has not made a statutory declaration of consent (if that is the case).

(9) If the application includes a statutory declaration of consent by the applicant's spouse, the Panel must give the spouse notice that the application has been made.

(10) If the Panel which is to determine the application requires information or evidence under subsection (6)(c) it must give reasons for doing so.".

Commencement Information

I21. Sch. 5 para. 19 in force at 30.6.2014 for specified purposes by S.I. 2014/1662, art. 2. (b)

I22. Sch. 5 para. 19 in force at 10.12.2014 in so far as not already in force by S.I. 2014/3169, art. 2

Membership of Panels determining applications on alternative grounds

20. Schedule 1 (Gender Recognition Panels), paragraph 4: after sub-paragraph (2) insert—
"(3)But a Panel need not include a medical member when determining an application under section 1. (1)(a) for a certificate to be granted in accordance with section 3. A.".

Commencement Information

I23. Sch. 5 para. 20 in force at 10.12.2014 by S.I. 2014/3169, art. 2

Schedule 6. Marriage overseas

Section 13

PART 1 Consular marriage under UK law

Provision for consular marriage

1. (1)Her Majesty may by Order in Council make provision for two people to marry each other—

(a) in prescribed countries or territories outside the United Kingdom, and

(b) in the presence of a registration officer,

in cases where the officer is satisfied that the conditions in sub-paragraph (2) are met.

(2) The conditions are that—

(a) at least one of the people proposing to marry is a United Kingdom national,

(b) the people proposing to marry would have been eligible to marry each other in such part of the United Kingdom as is determined in accordance with the Order,

(c) the authorities of the country or territory in which it is proposed that they marry will not object to the marriage, and

(d) insufficient facilities exist for them to enter into a marriage under the law of that country or territory.

Commencement Information

I1. Sch. 6 para. 1 in force at 21.1.2014 for specified purposes by S.I. 2014/93, art. 2. (b)(i)

I2. Sch. 6 para. 1 in force at 3.6.2014 in so far as not already in force by S.I. 2014/93, art. 5. (c)

Refusal by registration officer

2. (1)A registration officer is not required to allow two people to marry each other if the registration officer's opinion is that a marriage between them would be inconsistent with international law or the comity of nations.

(2) An Order in Council under this Part of this Schedule may make provision for appeals against a refusal, in reliance on sub-paragraph (1), to allow two people to marry each other.

Commencement Information

I3. Sch. 6 para. 2 in force at 21.1.2014 for specified purposes by S.I. 2014/93, art. 2. (b)(i)

I4. Sch. 6 para. 2 in force at 3.6.2014 in so far as not already in force by S.I. 2014/93, art. 5. (c)

No religious service

3. No religious service is to be used at the solemnization of a consular marriage.

Commencement Information

I5. Sch. 6 para. 3 in force at 3.6.2014 by S.I. 2014/93, art. 5. (c)

Treatment of marriage as taking place in part of UK for certain purposes

4. An Order in Council under this Part of this Schedule may provide that two people who marry in a consular marriage are to be treated for prescribed purposes as if they had married in the relevant part of the United Kingdom.

Commencement Information

I6. Sch. 6 para. 4 in force at 21.1.2014 for specified purposes by S.I. 2014/93, art. 2. (b)(ii)

I7. Sch. 6 para. 4 in force at 3.6.2014 in so far as not already in force by S.I. 2014/93, art. 5. (c)

Validity of consular marriage

5. A consular marriage is valid in law as if the marriage had been solemnized in the relevant part of the United Kingdom with a due observance of all forms required by the law of the relevant part of the United Kingdom.

Commencement Information

I8. Sch. 6 para. 5 in force at 3.6.2014 by S.I. 2014/93, art. 5. (c)

Interpretation

6. In this Part of this Schedule—

"consular marriage" means a marriage solemnized in accordance with the provisions of this Part of this Schedule and any Order in Council made under it;

"registration officer" means—
   - a consular officer in the service of Her Majesty's government in the United Kingdom, or
   - in the case of registration in a country or territory in which Her Majesty's government in the United Kingdom has for the time being no consular representative, a person authorised by the Secretary of State in respect of the solemnization of marriages in that country or territory;
"relevant part of the United Kingdom", in relation to a consular marriage, means the part of the United Kingdom determined in accordance with paragraph 1. (2)(b) for the purposes of the marriage.
Commencement Information
I9. Sch. 6 para. 6 in force at 21.1.2014 for specified purposes by S.I. 2014/93, art. 2. (b)(iii)
I10. Sch. 6 para. 6 in force at 3.6.2014 in so far as not already in force by S.I. 2014/93, art. 5. (c)

PART 2 Marriage under foreign law: certificates of no impediment

Provision for certificates of no impediment

7. (1)Her Majesty may by Order in Council make provision for the issue of certificates of no impediment to—
(a) United Kingdom nationals, and
(b) such other persons as may be prescribed,
who wish to marry in prescribed countries or territories outside the United Kingdom.
(2) A certificate of no impediment is a certificate that no legal impediment to the recipient entering into the marriage has been shown to the person issuing the certificate to exist.
Commencement Information
I11. Sch. 6 para. 7 in force at 21.1.2014 for specified purposes by S.I. 2014/93, art. 2. (b)(iii)
I12. Sch. 6 para. 7 in force at 3.6.2014 in so far as not already in force by S.I. 2014/93, art. 5. (c)

PART 3 Marriage of forces personnel under UK law

Provision for marriage of armed forces personnel

8. (1)Her Majesty may by Order in Council make provision for—
(a) a man and a woman to marry each other in any country or territory outside the United Kingdom, and
(b) for a same sex couple to marry in prescribed countries or territories outside the United Kingdom,
in the presence of an authorised person, in cases where the authorised person is satisfied that the conditions in sub-paragraph (2) are met.
(2) The conditions are that—
(a) at least one of the people proposing to marry is—
(i) a member of Her Majesty's forces serving in the country or territory in which it is proposed that they marry,
(ii) a relevant civilian who is employed in that country or territory, or
(iii) a child of a person falling within sub-paragraph (i) or (ii) whose home is with that person in that country or territory, and
(b) the people proposing to marry would have been eligible to marry each other in such part of the United Kingdom as is determined in accordance with the Order.
(3) In a case where one person ("P") treats, or has treated, another person ("C"), as a child of the

family in relation to—

(a) a marriage to which P is or was a party, or

(b) a civil partnership to which P is or was a party,

C is to be regarded for the purposes of sub-paragraph (2)(a)(iii) as the child of P.

Commencement Information

I13. Sch. 6 para. 8 in force at 21.1.2014 for specified purposes by S.I. 2014/93, art. 2. (b)(iii)

I14. Sch. 6 para. 8 in force at 3.6.2014 in so far as not already in force by S.I. 2014/93, art. 5. (c)

Religious services at forces marriages of same sex couples

9. (1)An Order in Council under this Part of this Schedule may make provision about the solemnization of forces marriages of same sex couples according to religious rites and usages.

(2) An Order in Council may, in particular, make provision—

(a) prohibiting the solemnization of such marriages according to particular religious rites or usages; or

(b) permitting the solemnization of such marriages according to particular religious rites or usages.

(3) Sub-paragraph (2)(b) is subject to sub-paragraphs (4) and (5).

(4) An Order in Council may not make provision allowing the solemnization of forces marriages of same sex couples according to the rites of the Church of England or Church in Wales.

(5) If an Order in Council makes provision allowing the solemnization of forces marriages of same sex couples according to particular religious rites or usages (other than those of the Church of England or Church in Wales), the Order in Council must also make provision to secure that such a marriage may not be solemnized according to those rites or usages unless the relevant governing authority has given written consent to marriages of same sex couples.

(6) The person or persons who are the relevant governing body for that purpose are to be determined in accordance with provision made by an Order in Council under this Part of this Schedule.

(7) This paragraph does not affect the provision that may be made about the solemnization of forces marriages of opposite sex couples according to religious rites and usages.

(8) If section 8 applies, the Lord Chancellor may, by order, make such relevant amending provision as the Lord Chancellor considers appropriate to allow for the solemnization of forces marriages of same sex couples according to the rites of the Church in Wales.

(9) For that purpose "relevant amending provision" means—

(a) provision amending sub-paragraphs (4) and (5) by omitting the words "or Church in Wales";

(b) provision amending any Order in Council made under this Part of this Schedule;

(c) provision amending any other UK legislation (including legislation contained in this Part of this Schedule).

(10) In making an order under sub-paragraph (8), the Lord Chancellor must have regard to the terms of the resolution of the Governing Body of the Church in Wales referred to in section 8. (1).

Commencement Information

I15. Sch. 6 para. 9 in force at 21.1.2014 for specified purposes by S.I. 2014/93, art. 2. (b)(iii)

I16. Sch. 6 para. 9 in force at 3.6.2014 in so far as not already in force by S.I. 2014/93, art. 5. (c)

Treatment of marriage as taking place in part of UK for certain purposes

10. An Order in Council under this Part of this Schedule may provide that two people who marry in a forces marriage are to be treated for prescribed purposes as if they had married in the relevant part of the United Kingdom.

Commencement Information

I17. Sch. 6 para. 10 in force at 21.1.2014 for specified purposes by S.I. 2014/93, art. 2. (b)(iii)

Validity of forces marriage

11. A forces marriage is valid in law as if the marriage had been solemnized in the relevant part of the United Kingdom with a due observance of all forms required by the law of the relevant part of the United Kingdom.

Commencement Information

I19. Sch. 6 para. 11 in force at 3.6.2014 by S.I. 2014/93, art. 5. (c)

Interpretation

12. (1)In this Part of this Schedule—
(a) a reference to a country or territory includes a reference to the waters of a country or territory;
(b) a reference to Her Majesty's forces serving in a country or territory includes a reference to such forces serving in a ship in the waters of a country or territory;
(c) a reference to a relevant civilian employed in a country or territory includes a reference to such a civilian employed in a ship in the waters of a country or territory.
(2) In this Part of this Schedule—
"authorised person", in relation to a marriage in a country or territory outside the United Kingdom, means—
    - a chaplain serving in any of Her Majesty's forces in that country or territory, or
    - a person authorised by the commanding officer of any of Her Majesty's forces in that country or territory to conduct that marriage or marriages generally;
"commanding officer" has the same meaning as in the Armed Forces Act 2006;
"forces marriage" means a marriage solemnized in accordance with the provisions of this Part of this Schedule and any Order in Council made under it;
"Her Majesty's forces" has the same meaning as in the Armed Forces Act 2006;
"relevant civilian" means a civilian subject to service discipline (within the meaning of the Armed Forces Act 2006) who is of a prescribed description;
"relevant part of the United Kingdom", in relation to a forces marriage, means the part of the United Kingdom determined in accordance with paragraph 8. (2)(b) for the purposes of the marriage.

Commencement Information

I20. Sch. 6 para. 12 in force at 21.1.2014 for specified purposes by S.I. 2014/93, art. 2. (b)(iv)
I21. Sch. 6 para. 12 in force at 3.6.2014 in so far as not already in force by S.I. 2014/93, art. 5. (c)

PART 4 General provisions

Parliamentary scrutiny

13. (1)No recommendation is to be made to Her Majesty in Council to make an Order in Council under this Schedule unless a draft of the statutory instrument containing the Order in Council has been laid before, and approved by resolution of, each House of Parliament.
(2) In the case of an Order in Council containing provision which would (if contained in an Act of the Scottish Parliament) be within the legislative competence of that Parliament, no recommendation is to be made to Her Majesty under this paragraph unless the Scottish Ministers have been consulted.

Commencement Information

I22. Sch. 6 para. 13 in force at 21.1.2014 for specified purposes by S.I. 2014/93, art. 2. (b)(iv)

123. Sch. 6 para. 13 in force at 3.6.2014 in so far as not already in force by S.I. 2014/93, art. 5. (c)

Particular kinds of provision

14. (1)An Order in Council under this Schedule may—
(a) make different provision for different purposes,
(b) make transitional, transitory or saving provision, or
(c) make consequential provision.
(2) An Order in Council under this Schedule may make provision corresponding to, or applying (with or without modifications), any UK legislation.
(3) An Order in Council under this Schedule may amend, repeal or revoke UK legislation.
Commencement Information
I24. Sch. 6 para. 14 in force at 21.1.2014 for specified purposes by S.I. 2014/93, art. 2. (b)(iv)
I25. Sch. 6 para. 14 in force at 3.6.2014 in so far as not already in force by S.I. 2014/93, art. 5. (c)

Interpretation

15. In this Schedule—
"prescribed" means prescribed by an Order in Council made under this Schedule;
"United Kingdom national" means a person who is—
  - a British citizen, a British overseas territories citizen, a British Overseas citizen or a British National (Overseas),
  - a British subject under the British Nationality Act 1981, or
  - a British protected person, within the meaning of that Act.
Commencement Information
I26. Sch. 6 para. 15 in force at 21.1.2014 for specified purposes by S.I. 2014/93, art. 2. (b)(iv)
I27. Sch. 6 para. 15 in force at 3.6.2014 in so far as not already in force by S.I. 2014/93, art. 5. (c)

Schedule 7. Transitional and consequential provision etc

Section 17

PART 1 Transitional and transitory provision

Approval of premises for civil weddings

1. (1)The approved premises regulations, and any related guidance, that are in force immediately before commencement have effect after commencement in relation to marriage in pursuance of section 26. (1)(bb) of the Marriage Act 1949 as amended by this Act.
(2) Any approval of premises under those regulations that is in force immediately before commencement has effect after commencement in relation to marriage in pursuance of section 26. (1)(bb) of the Marriage Act 1949 as amended by this Act.
(3) Any application for approval of premises made under approved premises regulations before commencement continues to have effect after commencement as an application for the approval of the premises for the purposes of marriage in pursuance of section 26. (1)(bb) of the Marriage Act 1949 as amended by this Act.

(4) In this paragraph—

"approved premises regulations" means regulations under section 46. A of the Marriage Act 1949;

"commencement" means the time when section 1 comes into force;

"related guidance" means any guidance relating to premises approved under approved premises regulations.

Commencement Information

I1. Sch. 7 para. 1 in force at 13.3.2014 by S.I. 2014/93, art. 3. (k)(i)

PART 2 Minor and consequential amendments

Marriage Act 1949 (c. 76)

2. The Marriage Act 1949 is amended as follows.

Commencement Information

I2. Sch. 7 para. 2 in force at 13.3.2014 by S.I. 2014/93, art. 3. (k)(i)

3. Section 3 (marriages of persons under 18), subsection (1): after "widow" insert " or a surviving civil partner ".

Commencement Information

I3. Sch. 7 para. 3 in force at 13.3.2014 by S.I. 2014/93, art. 3. (k)(i)

4. (1)Section 25 (void marriages) is amended as follows.

(2) At the beginning insert—

"(1)A marriage shall be void in any of the following cases.".

(3) The existing wording of section 25 becomes subsection (2) of that section; and, at the beginning of that subsection, for "If any persons" substitute—

"(2)Case A is where any persons".

(4) For the words after paragraph (d) substitute—

"(3)Case B is where any persons knowingly and wilfully consent to or acquiesce in the solemnization of a Church of England marriage between them by a person who is not in Holy Orders.

(4) Case C is where any persons of the same sex consent to or acquiesce in the solemnization of a Church of England marriage between them.

(5) In subsections (3) and (4) "Church of England marriage" means a marriage according to the rites of the Church of England.".

Commencement Information

I4. Sch. 7 para. 4 in force at 13.3.2014 by S.I. 2014/93, art. 3. (k)(i)

5. Section 27. A (additional information required in certain cases), subsection (1): after "section 26. (1)(dd)" insert " or 26. B(6) ".

Commencement Information

I5. Sch. 7 para. 5 in force at 13.3.2014 by S.I. 2014/93, art. 3. (k)(i)

6. After section 27. C insert—

"27. DAdditional information required for certain marriages of same sex couples

(1) This section applies in relation to any marriage intended to be solemnized in pursuance of section 26. B(2), (4) or (6) (marriage of same sex couples: Quaker marriage, Jewish marriage, marriage of house-bound or detained person).

(2) The superintendent registrar to whom notice of such a marriage is given under section 27 may require the relevant governing authority to provide a copy of the consent mentioned in section 26. B(2)(b), (4)(b) or (6)(d).

(3) In this section, "relevant governing authority", in relation to an intended marriage under section 26. B(2), (4) or (6), has the same meaning as in that provision.".

Commencement Information

I6. Sch. 7 para. 6 in force at 13.3.2014 by S.I. 2014/93, art. 3. (k)(i)

7. (1)Section 28. A (power to require evidence) is amended in accordance with this paragraph.

(2) After subsection (1) insert—

"(1. A)In the case of an intended marriage to which section 27. D applies, the superintendent registrar to whom the notice of the marriage is given may require the relevant governing authority to produce evidence relating to the consent mentioned in section 26. B(2)(b), (4)(b) or (6)(d).".

(3) Subsection (2): for "Such a requirement" substitute " A requirement under subsection (1) or (1. A) ".

Commencement Information

I7. Sch. 7 para. 7 in force at 13.3.2014 by S.I. 2014/93, art. 3. (k)(i)

8. (1)Section 41 (registration of buildings) is amended in accordance with this paragraph.

(2) The title: at the end insert " : marriage of a man and a woman ".

(3) After subsection (1) insert—

"(1. A)A reference in this section to the solemnization of marriage is a reference to the solemnization of marriage of a man and a woman.".

Commencement Information

I8. Sch. 7 para. 8 in force at 13.3.2014 by S.I. 2014/93, art. 3. (k)(i)

9. (1)Section 42 (cancellation of registration and substitution of another building) is amended in accordance with this paragraph.

(2) For the title substitute " Cancellation of registration under section 41: building no longer used ".

(3) Subsection (1): for "registered building" substitute " building registered under section 41 ".

Commencement Information

I9. Sch. 7 para. 9 in force at 13.3.2014 by S.I. 2014/93, art. 3. (k)(i)

10. (1)Section 43 (appointment of authorised persons) is amended in accordance with this paragraph.

(2) For the title substitute " Buildings registered under section 41: appointment of authorised persons ".

(3) Subsection (1): for "registered building" (in each place) substitute " building registered under section 41 ".

(4) For the proviso to subsection (1) substitute—

"(1. A)The power conferred by this section may only be exercised after the end of the relevant one year period (and, if that period has ended before the date of the registration under section 41, the power may accordingly be exercised immediately).

(1. B)The relevant one year period is the period of one year beginning with the date of the registration of the building under section 41 (the "new registration").

(1. C)But if—

    (a) there is any earlier registration of the building under section 43. A which is still in force at the date of the new registration, or

    (b) there has been any earlier qualifying registration of a previous building,

the relevant one year period is the period of one year beginning with the date of that registration (or the earlier of those dates).

(1. D)For that purpose there is a qualifying registration of a previous building if—

    (a) the congregation on whose behalf the new registration is made previously used another building for the purpose of public religious worship,

    (b) that building was registered under section 41 or 43. A, and

    (c) that registration was cancelled not more than one month before the date of the new registration.".

(5) Omit subsection (2).

Commencement Information

I10. Sch. 7 para. 10 in force at 13.3.2014 by S.I. 2014/93, art. 3. (k)(i)

11. Section 44 (solemnization of marriage in registered building), subsection (2)(b): for "the last foregoing section" substitute " section 43 (in the case of the marriage of a man and a woman), or section 43. B (in the case of the marriage of a same sex couple), ".

55

Commencement Information
I11. Sch. 7 para. 11 in force at 13.3.2014 by S.I. 2014/93, art. 3. (k)(i)

12. Section 45. A (solemnization of certain marriages), subsection (1): after "section 26. (1)(dd)" insert " or 26. B(6) ".

Commencement Information
I12. Sch. 7 para. 12 in force at 13.3.2014 by S.I. 2014/93, art. 3. (k)(i)

13. (1)Section 46 (register office marriage followed by religious ceremony) is amended in accordance with this paragraph.

(2) Subsection (1): for "marriage solemnised in the presence of a superintendent registrar" substitute " relevant marriage ".

(3) After subsection (1) insert—

"(1. A)In this section "relevant marriage" means—

  (a) the marriage of a man and a woman solemnized in the presence of a superintendent registrar,

  (b) the marriage of a same sex couple solemnized in the presence of a superintendent registrar, and

  (c) a marriage which arises from the conversion of a civil partnership under regulations under section 9 of the Marriage (Same Sex Couples) Act 2013.

(1. B)This section does not authorise the marriage service of the Church of England to be read or celebrated in the case of a relevant marriage of a same sex couple.

(1. C)This section does not authorise any other marriage service to be read or celebrated in the case of a relevant marriage of a same sex couple unless the relevant governing authority has given written consent to the reading or celebration of that service in the case of such marriages.

(1. D)For that purpose—

"relevant governing authority" means the person or persons recognised by the members of the relevant religious organisation as competent for the purpose of giving consent for the purposes of this section;

"relevant religious organisation" means the religious organisation whose marriage service is to be read or celebrated.".

Commencement Information
I13. Sch. 7 para. 13 in force at 13.3.2014 by S.I. 2014/93, art. 3. (k)(i)

14. Section 48 (proof of certain matters not necessary to validity of marriages), subsection (1)—

(a) paragraph (d): omit "or";

(b) after paragraph (d) insert—

  "(da)that, in the case of a marriage under section 26. B(2), (4) or (6), the relevant governing authority had given consent as mentioned in section 26. B(2)(b), (4)(b) or (6)(d);";

(c) at the end of paragraph (e) insert "or

  (ea) that, in the case of a marriage under section 26. A, the relevant governing authority had given consent as mentioned in section 26. A(3);".

Commencement Information
I14. Sch. 7 para. 14 in force at 13.3.2014 by S.I. 2014/93, art. 3. (k)(i)

15. After section 49 insert—

"49. AVoid marriages: additional provision about same sex couples

(1) If a same sex couple knowingly and wilfully intermarries under the provisions of this Part of this Act in the absence of the required consent, the marriage shall be void.

(2) In this section, in relation to a marriage of a same sex couple, "required consent" means consent under—

  (a) section 26. A(3), in a case where section 26. A applies to the marriage (but section 44. A does not apply to it);

  (b) section 26. A(3) and section 44. A(6), in a case where section 26. A and section 44. A apply to the marriage;

  (c) section 26. B(2)(b), in a case where section 26. B(1), (2) and (3) apply to the marriage;

  (d) section 26. B(4)(b), in a case where section 26. B(1), (4) and (5) apply to the marriage;

  (e) section 26. B(6)(d), in a case where section 26. B(1), (6) and (7) apply to the marriage.".

Commencement Information
I15. Sch. 7 para. 15 in force at 13.3.2014 by S.I. 2014/93, art. 3. (k)(i)
16. Section 53, paragraph (c): for the words from "religion" to the end substitute "religion—
(i) where the parties to the marriage are both members of the same synagogue, the marriage shall be registered by the secretary of that synagogue; and
(ii) where the parties to the marriage are members of different synagogues, the marriage shall be registered by the secretary of whichever of those synagogues the parties to the marriage nominate;".
Commencement Information
I16. Sch. 7 para. 16 in force at 13.3.2014 by S.I. 2014/93, art. 3. (k)(i)
17. Section 69 (licensing of chapels for marriages according to rites of Church of England), subsection (5): for "authorised persons" substitute " persons authorised under section 43 ".
Commencement Information
I17. Sch. 7 para. 17 in force at 13.3.2014 by S.I. 2014/93, art. 3. (k)(i)
18. Section 70 (registration of chapels for marriages otherwise than according to rites of Church of England), subsection (1), paragraphs (a) and (b): for "registered building" substitute " building registered under section 41 ".
Commencement Information
I18. Sch. 7 para. 18 in force at 13.3.2014 by S.I. 2014/93, art. 3. (k)(i)
19. (1)Section 75 (offences relating to solemnization of marriages) is amended in accordance with this paragraph.
(2) Subsection (2)(bb): after "section 26. (1)(dd)" insert " or 26. B(6) ".
(3) Subsection (3)(d): after "(dd)" insert " or 26. B(6) ".
(4) Subsection (5): after "seventy" insert " or 70. A ".
Commencement Information
I19. Sch. 7 para. 19 in force at 13.3.2014 by S.I. 2014/93, art. 3. (k)(i)
20. (1)Section 78 (interpretation) is amended in accordance with this paragraph.
(2) Subsection (1)—
(a) for the definition of "authorised person" substitute—
""authorised person" means—
    (a) in relation to a building registered under section 41, a person whose name and address have been certified in accordance with section 43;
    (b) in relation to a building registered under section 43. A, a person whose name and address have been certified in accordance with section 43. B;";
(b) after the definition of "ecclesiastical district" insert—
""England and Wales legislation" has the same meaning as in the Marriage (Same Sex Couples) Act 2013;";
(c) definition of "registered building": for "Part III" substitute " section 41 or section 43. A ".
(3) After subsection (5) insert—
"(6)If, for the purpose of any provision of this Act, a relevant governing authority has given written consent to marriages of same sex couples, the validity of that consent is not affected only because there is a change in the person or persons constituting that relevant governing authority.".
Commencement Information
I20. Sch. 7 para. 20 in force at 13.3.2014 by S.I. 2014/93, art. 3. (k)(i)
21. (1)Schedule 4 (provisions of Act which are excluded or modified in their application to Naval, Military and Air Force chapels) is amended in accordance with this paragraph.
(2) Part 3 (exclusion of provisions relating to marriages otherwise than according to the rites of the Church of England): after the entry relating to section 43 insert— " Sections 43. A and 43. C. ".
(3) Part 4 (modification of provisions relating to marriages otherwise than according to the rites of the Church of England), after "forty-three," insert " 43. B, ".
Commencement Information
I21. Sch. 7 para. 21 in force at 3.6.2014 by S.I. 2014/93, art. 5. (d)

Marriage (Registrar General's Licence) Act 1970.

22. The Marriage (Registrar General's Licence) Act 1970 is amended as follows.
Commencement Information
I22. Sch. 7 para. 22 in force at 13.3.2014 by S.I. 2014/93, art. 3. (k)(ii)
23. Section 1 (marriages which may be solemnized by Registrar General's licence), subsection (2): after "section 26. (1)(dd)" insert " or 26. B(6) ".
Commencement Information
I23. Sch. 7 para. 23 in force at 13.3.2014 by S.I. 2014/93, art. 3. (k)(ii)
24. Section 2 (notice of marriage), after subsection (3) insert—
"(4)Sections 27. D and 28. A(1. A) and (2) of the principal Act apply (with the appropriate modifications) to a marriage intended to be solemnized in pursuance of this Act as they apply to a marriage intended to be solemnized in pursuance of 26. B(2), (4) or (6) of that Act.".
Commencement Information
I24. Sch. 7 para. 24 in force at 13.3.2014 by S.I. 2014/93, art. 3. (k)(ii)
25. After section 13 insert—
"13. AVoid marriages: additional provision about same sex couples
(1) If a same sex couple knowingly and wilfully intermarries under the provisions of this Act in the absence of the required consent, the marriage shall be void.
(2) In this section "required consent" means consent under section 1. (3).".
Commencement Information
I25. Sch. 7 para. 25 in force at 13.3.2014 by S.I. 2014/93, art. 3. (k)(ii)

Matrimonial Causes Act 1973 (c. 18)

26. The Matrimonial Causes Act 1973 is amended as follows.
Commencement Information
I26. Sch. 7 para. 26 in force at 13.3.2014 by S.I. 2014/93, art. 3. (k)(ii)
27. Section 11 (grounds on which a marriage is void): omit paragraph (c).
Commencement Information
I27. Sch. 7 para. 27 in force at 13.3.2014 by S.I. 2014/93, art. 3. (k)(ii)

Public Order Act 1986 (c. 64)

28. (1)Section 29. JA of the Public Order Act 1986 (protection of freedom of expression (sexual orientation)) is amended in accordance with this paragraph.
(2) The existing provision of section 29. JA becomes subsection (1) of that section.
(3) After that provision insert—
"(2)In this Part, for the avoidance of doubt, any discussion or criticism of marriage which concerns the sex of the parties to marriage shall not be taken of itself to be threatening or intended to stir up hatred.".
Commencement Information
I28. Sch. 7 para. 28 in force at 13.3.2014 by S.I. 2014/93, art. 3. (k)(ii)

Social Security Contributions and Benefits Act 1992 (c. 4)

29[F1. The Social Security Contributions and Benefits Act 1992 is amended as follows.]
Amendments (Textual)
F1. Sch. 7 para. 30 repealed (S.) (16.12.2014) by The Marriage and Civil Partnership (Scotland) Act 2014 and Civil Partnership Act 2004 (Consequential Provisions and Modifications) Order 2014 (S.I. 2014/3229), art. 1. (2), Sch. 5 para. 21

Commencement Information
I29. Sch. 7 para. 29 in force at 10.12.2014 by S.I. 2014/3169, art. 2

30[F1. Section 48 (use of former spouse's or civil partner's contributions): after subsection (4) insert—

"(5)For the purposes of this section, a civil partnership is not to be treated as having terminated by reason of its having been converted into a marriage under section 9 of the Marriage (Same Sex Couples) Act 2013.".]

Amendments (Textual)

F1. Sch. 7 para. 30 repealed (S.) (16.12.2014) by The Marriage and Civil Partnership (Scotland) Act 2014 and Civil Partnership Act 2004 (Consequential Provisions and Modifications) Order 2014 (S.I. 2014/3229), art. 1. (2), Sch. 5 para. 21

Commencement Information
I30. Sch. 7 para. 30 in force at 10.12.2014 by S.I. 2014/3169, art. 2

Pension Schemes Act 1993 (c. 48)

31. The Pension Schemes Act 1993 is amended as follows.

Commencement Information
I31. Sch. 7 para. 31 in force at 13.3.2014 by S.I. 2014/93, art. 3. (k)(iii)

32. Section 99 (trustees' duties after exercise of option), subsection (3)(b): for "his widow" substitute " his or her surviving spouse or civil partner ".

Commencement Information
I32. Sch. 7 para. 32 in force at 13.3.2014 by S.I. 2014/93, art. 3. (k)(iii)

Civil Partnership Act 2004 (c. 33)

33. The Civil Partnership Act 2004 is amended as follows.

Commencement Information
I33. Sch. 7 para. 33 in force at 13.3.2014 by S.I. 2014/93, art. 3. (k)(iii)

34. Section 1 (civil partnership), subsection (3)—

(a) after "only" insert " (a) ";

(b) after "annulment" insert ", or

(b) in the case of a civil partnership formed as mentioned in subsection (1)(a)(i) or (iv), on the conversion of the civil partnership into a marriage under section 9 of the Marriage (Same Sex Couples) Act 2013.".

Commencement Information
I34. Sch. 7 para. 34 in force at 10.12.2014 by S.I. 2014/3169, art. 2

35. Section 4 (parental etc consent where proposed civil partner under 18), subsection (3): after "partner" insert " or a widower or a widow ".

Commencement Information
I35. Sch. 7 para. 35 in force at 13.3.2014 by S.I. 2014/93, art. 3. (k)(iv)

36. Section 210 (registration at British consulates etc), subsection (6), paragraph (b) of the definition of "Registration officer": after "country" (in both places) insert " or territory ".

Commencement Information
I36. Sch. 7 para. 36 in force at 13.3.2014 by S.I. 2014/93, art. 3. (k)(iv)

Human Fertilisation and Embryology Act 2008 (c. 22)

37. The Human Fertilisation and Embryology Act 2008 is amended as follows.

Commencement Information
I37. Sch. 7 para. 37 in force at 13.3.2014 by S.I. 2014/93, art. 3. (k)(iv)

38. (1)Section 35 (woman married at time of treatment) is amended in accordance with this paragraph.

(2) The title: after "married" insert " to a man ".

(3) Subsection (1)(a): after "marriage" insert " with a man ".

Commencement Information

I38. Sch. 7 para. 38 in force at 13.3.2014 by S.I. 2014/93, art. 3. (k)(iv)

39. Section 40 (embryo transferred after death of husband etc who did not provide sperm), subsection (1)(b): after "marriage" insert " with a man ".

Commencement Information

I39. Sch. 7 para. 39 in force at 13.3.2014 by S.I. 2014/93, art. 3. (k)(iv)

40. (1)Section 42 (woman in civil partnership at time of treatment) is amended in accordance with this paragraph.

(2) The title: after "partnership" insert " or marriage to a woman ".

(3) Subsection (1)—

(a) after "partnership" (in the first place) insert " or a marriage with another woman ";

(b) after "partnership" (in the second place) insert " or marriage ".

Commencement Information

I40. Sch. 7 para. 40 in force at 13.3.2014 by S.I. 2014/93, art. 3. (k)(iv)

41. (1)Section 46 (embryo transferred after death of civil partner or intended female parent) is amended in accordance with this paragraph.

(2) The title: after "civil partner" insert " or wife ".

(3) Subsection (1)—

(a) paragraph (b), after "partnership" insert " or marriage with another woman ";

(b) paragraphs (c), (d) and (e), after "partnership" insert " or marriage ";

(c) the words after paragraph (f), after "partnership" insert " or marriage ".

Commencement Information

I41. Sch. 7 para. 41 in force at 13.3.2014 by S.I. 2014/93, art. 3. (k)(iv)

Equality Act 2010 (c. 15)

42. The Equality Act 2010 is amended as follows.

Commencement Information

I42. Sch. 7 para. 42 in force at 13.3.2014 by S.I. 2014/93, art. 3. (k)(iv)

43. (1)Section 23 (comparison by reference to circumstances) is amended in accordance with this paragraph.

(2) Subsection (3): after "married" insert " to a person of the opposite sex ".

(3) After subsection (3) insert—

"(4)If the protected characteristic is sexual orientation, the fact that one person (whether or not the person referred to as B) is married to a person of the same sex while another is married to a person of the opposite sex is not a material difference between the circumstances relating to each case.".

Commencement Information

I43. Sch. 7 para. 43 in force at 13.3.2014 by S.I. 2014/93, art. 3. (k)(iv)

44. Schedule 3 (services and public functions: exceptions): for the title to Part 6 substitute— " Marriage: gender reassignment ".

Commencement Information

I44. Sch. 7 para. 44 in force at 13.3.2014 by S.I. 2014/93, art. 3. (k)(iv)

45. Schedule 9 (work: exceptions), Part 1 (occupational requirements), paragraph 2 (religious requirements relating to sex, marriage etc, sexual orientation), sub-paragraph (4): after paragraph (c) insert—

"(ca)a requirement not to be married to a person of the same sex;".

Commencement Information

I45. Sch. 7 para. 45 in force at 13.3.2014 by S.I. 2014/93, art. 3. (k)(iv)

Open Government Licence v3.0

Contains public sector information licensed under the Open Government Licence v3.0.
The full licence if available at the following address:
http://www.nationalarchives.gov.uk/doc/open-government-licence/version/3/

Printed in Great Britain
by Amazon

20190869R00038